Egyptian Book of the Dead and the Ancient Mysteries of Amenta

All Rights reserved. No part of this book maybe reproduced without written permission from the publishers, except by a reviewer who may quote brief passages in a review to be printed in a newspaper or magazine.

Printed January, 2014

Published and Distributed By:

Lushena Books
607 Country Club Drive, Unit E
Bensenville, IL 60106
www.lushenabks.com

ISBN: 978-1-63182-995-6

Printed in the United States of America

Egyptian Book of the Dead and the Ancient Mysteries of Amenta

by

Gerald Massey

ISBN: 978-1-63182-675-7

Gerald Massey

EGYPTIAN BOOK OF THE DEAD AND THE MYSTERIES OF AMENTA

From:

Gerald Massey's Lecturtes

**Egyptian Book of the Dead
and the Mysteries of Amenta**

EGYPTIAN BOOK OF THE DEAD AND THE MYSTERIES OF AMENTA

The Egyptian Book of the Dead contains the oldest known religious writings in the world. As it comes to us it is mainly Osirian, but the Osirian group of gods was the latest of all the divine dynasties, although these, as shown at Abydos (by Prof. Flinders Petrie), will account for some ten thousand years of time in Egypt. The antiquity of the collection is not to be judged by the age of the coffins in which the papyrus rolls were found. Amongst other criteria of length in time the absence of Amen, Maut, and Khunsu supplies a gauge. The presence and importance of Tum affords another, whilst the persistence of Apt and her son Sebek–Horus tells a tale of times incalculably remote.

As a key to the mysteries and the method of the book it must be understood at starting that the eschatology or doctrine of Last Things was founded in the mould of the mythology, and that the one can only be unravelled by means of the other. Moreover, there is plenty of evidence to prove that the Ritual was based on the mythology, and not the mythology upon the Ritual. The serpent, of darkness, was the evil reptile in mythology. In theology it becomes the deluder of mankind. Here the beginning was with darkness itself, which was the deceiver from the first. The serpent, being a figure of darkness, was continued by theology as the official adversary of souls in the eschatological domain. The eschatology of the Ritual, then, can only be comprehended by means of the mythology. And it is the mythos out of view that has made the Ritual so profoundly difficult to understand. Reading it may be compared with a dance seen by a deaf man who does not hear the music to which the motion is timed, and who has no clue to the characters being performed in the dumb drama. You cannot understand what they are doing and saying as Manes in another world without knowing what was thought and said by human beings in this concerning that representation of the nature powers, the gods and goddesses, which constitutes mythology.

Amenta is a huge fossil formation crowded with the dead forms of a past life in which the horny conspectuities of learned ignorance will only see dead shells for a modern museum. As a rule, Egypt is always treated differently from the rest of the world. No Egyptologist has ever dreamed that the Ritual still exists under the disguise of both the gnostic and canonical gospels, or that it was the fountain–head and source of all the books of wisdom claimed to be divine. In the mythology – that is, in the primitive mode of rendering the phenomena of external nature – Osiris as light-giver in the moon was tom in fourteen pieces during the latter half of the lunation by the evil Sut, the opposing power of darkness. He was put together again and reconstituted by his son, beloved Horus, the young solar god. This representation could not have been made until it was known that the lunar light was replenished monthly from the solar source. Then Horus as the sun god and the vanquisher of Sut, the power of darkness, could be called the reconstituter of Osiris in the moon. In that way a foundation was laid in natural fact according to the science of mythology, and a mystery bequeathed to the eschatology which is doctrinal. For as it had been with the dismembered, mutilated god in the mythos, so it is with the Osiris deceased, who has to be reconstructed for a future life and put together bit by bit as a spiritual body in one of the great mysteries of Amenta. In the mythos Har–Makhu was the solar god of both horizons, or the double equinox, who represented the sun of today that rose up from the nether world as conqueror of darkness to join the west and east together on the Mount of Glory, as the connecting link of continuity in time betwixt yesterday and tomorrow. The type was continued in the eschatology, when Har–Makhu became the Horus of the greater mysteries, Horus of the religious legend who suffered, died, and was buried in Amenta, and who rose again from ,the dead like the winter sun, as Horus in spirit, lifting aloft the insignia of his sovereignty. This was he who made the pathway, not merely betwixt the two horizons, but to eternal life, as son of Ra, the holy spirit in the eschatology. The intermediate link in the mythos, which "connects the solar orb with yesterday", is now the intermediary betwixt the two worlds and two lives in time and eternity. This is he who exclaims, "I am the link! I am the everlasting one! I am Horus who steppeth onwards through eternity."(Rit., ch. 42.) This was he who, in the words of the gnostic Paul, "broke down the wall of partition" and "made both one", "that he might create in himself one new man" and reconcile them both in one body", even as the double Horus, Har–Sam–Taui, was made one when blended and established as one person in another mystery of Amenta (Rit., ch. 42).

The mythology repeated in the Ritual is mainly solar and Osirian, but with glimpses of the lunar and the stellar mythos from the beginning. For example, Apt the ancient genetrix, as goddess of the Great Bear constellation, and leader of the heavenly host, was the kindler of the starry sparks by night in the mythology. In the eschatology she is continued as the mistress of divine protections for the soul, and she who had been the kindler of the lights in the darkness of night was now propitiated as rekindler of life from the spark in the dark of death (Rit., ch. 137B). Ra in the mythos is the solar god represented by the sun in heaven, and in the eschatology he became the god in spirit who is called the holy spirit and first person in the trinity which consisted of Atum the father god, Horus the son, and Ra the holy spirit; the three that were also one in the Osirian cult, first as three forms of the solar god and next as three forms of the god in spirit. It is thus we are enabled to trace the formation of the Egyptian eschatology in the mould of the mythology.

There is no death in the Osirian religion, only decay and change, and periodic renewal; only evolution and transformation in the domain of matter and the transubstantiation into spirit. In the so–called death of Osiris it is rebirth, not death, exactly the same as in the changes of external nature. At the close of day the solar orb went down and left the sun god staring blankly in the dark of death. Taht the moon god met him in Amenta with the eye of Horus as the light that was to illuminate the darkness of the subterranean world. In the annual rendering on the third day light was generated by renewal in the moon. Thus Osiris rose again, and a doctrine of the resurrection on the third day was bequeathed to the eschatology. The sun in sinking was buried as a body (or mummy) in the nether world of Amenta. When rising again at dawn it was transformed into a soul, a supreme elemental soul, that preceded the god in spirit. This was in the mythology. In the eschatology the same types were reapplied to the human soul, which was imaged in the flesh as the inarticulate, blind, and impubescent Horus, who died bodily but was preserved in mummy form to make his transformation into the luminous Sahu, when he rose again in glory as Horus the divine adult. "I am the resurrection and the life" is the perfect interpretation of an Egyptian picture that was copied by Denon at Philæ. (*Egypt*, vol. ii., pl.40, No.8, p. 54–) (Lundy, fig. 183.) Divine Horus is portrayed in the act of raising the deceased Osiris from the bier by presenting to him the Ankh sign of life. He was the life in person who performed the resurrection, and therefore is "*the resurrection and the life*". As such he simply stands for a soul considered to be the divine offspring of god the father, not for any historical character that makes preposterous pretensions to possess miraculous power. Previously he had been the resurrection and the life *as solar vivifier in the physical* domain, or otherwise stated in the mythology. It was this difference betwixt the mythology and eschatology that constituted the lesser and the greater mysteries. The lesser in their origin were partly sociological. They were the customs and the ceremonial rites of totemism. The greater mysteries are eschatological and religious. For instance, the transformation of the youth into the adult or the girl into a woman in the totemic mysteries was applied doctrinally to the transformation of the soul in the mysteries of Amenta. With the more primitive races, such as the Arunta of Australia, the mysteries remain chiefly totemic and sociological, though interfused with the religious sentiment. The greater mysteries were perfected in the Egyptian religion, to be read of in the Ritual as the mysteries of Amenta.

From the beginning to the end of the written Ritual we shall find it is based upon the mythical representation which was primary. The mythical representation was first applied to the phenomena of external nature, and this mode of representation was continued and re-applied to the human soul in the eschatology. Egyptian myths, then, are not inventions made to explain the Ritual. Totemic representation was earlier. This mode was continued in the mythology. Ritual arose from the rendering becoming religious in the phase of eschatology, and did not originate as an explanation of mythology and totemism. But not until the different phases are discriminated can the Ritual be read, that which has been founded on it under–stood, or the mental status of the thinkers ascertained. In the mythology the solar god, who in his primary form was Ptah (Khepr), is the maker of a complete circle for the sun as founder and opener of the nether earth, this solar pathway being a figure of for ever, a type of the eternal working in time. In the eschatology the god in spirit who is Ra the holy spirit is "the god who has created (or opened out) eternity" (Rit., ch. 15). The one is on the physical basis, the other on the spiritual plane. In the mythology the seven primordial powers that pass through various phases, elemental, stellar , or lunar, always in a group of seven, finally become the seven souls of Ra, who attained supremacy as the sun god in mythology and also as the holy spirit. Thence came the doctrine of the seven souls in man, as seven gifts of the holy spirit in the eschatology. In the mythical representation Sothis on New Year's Day was the bringer forth of the child that was mothered by Hathor or Isis. The type is employed in the eschatology of the Ritual when the Manes in Amenta prays for rebirth as a pure spirit and says, "May I live (or rise up and go forth) from between the closed knees of Sothis". The rebirth of the child in Sothis was the renewal of the year, Sothis being represented in the feminine character by Hathor as the bringer forth from betwixt her knees or, as elsewhere rendered, her kheptu, *i.e.*, her thighs. So the Manes are reborn from between the thighs of Nut in the mysteries of Amenta, and here the visible birthplace of spirits perfected is localized in Sothis, the opener of the year and bringer of the babe to birth upon the horizon or the mount of glory. In this way the skies of night were made luminous with starry lore that was mythical in the astronomy and the words of a divine wisdom in the later eschatology when the mysteries were represented in Amenta. Instead of flashlights showing pictures on the housetops of a city after dark, the stars were used by the Egyptians to illustrate the mysteries that were out of sight. The triumph of Horus over Sut or over the Apap dragon of drought and darkness was illustrated in the stellar mythos when in the annual round Orion rose and the Scorpion constellation set upon the opposite horizon. The Egyptian nearing death could lie and look upon a future figured in the starry heavens. As it was with Osiris or Horus so would it be with him. The way had been mapped out, the guiding stars were visible. His bier or coffin of new birth could be seen in the mesken of the mother. He rose again in spirit as the babe of Sothis. "He joined the company of the holy Sahus" in Orion with the pilot Horus at the look-out of the bark. He saw the golden isles in a heaven of perpetual peace to which the pole was the eternal mooring post. Whilst he was passing from this life the bark of Ra was making ready for his soul to go on board.

The foundation of Amenta itself has yet to be delineated. It is a tangible threshold to the other world, the secret but solid earth of eternity which was opened up by Ptah when he and his seven Khnemmu erected the Tat pillar that was founded in the winter solstice as the figure of a stability that was to be eternal. In the mythos the Tat is a type of the sun in the winter solstice that has the power of returning from the lowest depth and thus completing the eternal road. In the eschatology it is the god in person as Ptah-Sekeri or Osiris, the backbone and support of the universe. Horus erecting the Tat in Sekhem was raising Osiris from the sepulchre, the father re-erected as the son in the typical resurrection and continuity of the human spirit in the after life. The figure of Amsu-Horus rising in the resurrection or "coming forth", with member erect, has two characters, one in the mythology, one in the eschatology. In the mythology he images the phallus of the sun and the generative force that fecundates the Mother–earth. In the eschatology the image of erection is repeated as a symbol of resurrection, and in this phase the supposed phallic god, the figure of regenerative force, is typical of the resurrection or re–erection of the mortal in spirit.

Horus the child with finger to mouth is portrayed in the sign of the Scales at the autumn equinox, the point at which the sun begins to lessen and become impotent. This the Egyptians termed the "little sun", which when personified was infant Horus, who sank down into Hades as the suffering sun to die in the winter solstice and be transformed to rise again and return in all his glory and power in the equinox at Easter. This was matter of the solar mythos, also of life in vegetation and in the water of the inundation. In the eschatology Horus the child is typical of the human soul which was incarnated in the blood of Isis, the immaculate virgin, to be made flesh and to be born in mortal guise on earth as the son of Seb, and to suffer all the afflictions of mortality. He descended to Amenta as the soul sinking in the dark of death, and as the soul he was transfigured, changed, and glorified, to rise again and become immortal as a spirit perfected according to the teachings in the eschatology. A brief list will show how certain zootypes that were founded in the mythological representation were continued in the eschatology :

Type of power	Mythical	Eschatological
The beetle	= The sun as transformer	= The god as self–evolver
The serpent	= Renewal	= Eternal life
The ibis	= Messenger	= Word or logos
The jackal	= Seer in the dark	= Guide in death
The heifer	= The moon	= Virgin mother
The hawk	= Soul of the sun	= Ra the divine spirit
Fish, calf, or lamb	= Youthful solar god re–born	= The messiah

In the mythology the Apap reptile lies in the Lake of Darkness, where the sun goes down, as the eternal adversary of the light with which it is at war all night and all the winter through. He seeks to bar the way of the sun in the nether world. In the eschatology it is the human soul instead of the sun that has to struggle with the opposing monster in making the passage of Amenta. The same scenery served, as already shown, to illustrate the mystery in a religious and spiritual phase.

Chapter 64 of the Ritual is known to have been extant in the time of King Septi, of the first dynasty, the Usaiphais of Manetho. That was over 6,000 years ago. It is a chapter from the Book of Life "to be recited on coming forth to day, that one may not be kept back on the path of the Tuat, whether on entering or in coming forth; for taking all the forms which one desireth, and that the person may not die a second time". If this chapter be known, the person is made triumphant on earth (as in the nether world), and he performeth all things which are done by the living. The chapter was then so ancient that it had been lost sight of, and was discovered "on a plinth of the god of the Hennu (or Sekru) bark, by a master builder in the time of King Septi the Victorious". When this chapter was composed the primary nature powers had been unified in the one god, who was represented as the lord of two faces, who "seeth by his own light", the "Lord of Resurrections, who commeth forth from the dusk, and whose birth is from the House of Death". That is, as the solar god who was Atum on one horizon and Horus on the other; hence the lord of two faces. The supreme god thus described is the father in one character, the son in the other. The Manes speaking in the character of the son says of the father, "He is I, and I am he". At that time the earth had been tunnelled by Ptah and his pigmy workers, and a spirit world created on the new *terra firma* in the earth of eternity, over which the solar god effused his radiance nightly when he lighted up the Tuat with his indescribable glories (ch. 15). The "Lord of Resurrections" as a solar god had then become the lord of resurrections as the generator of ever–living souls. Egyptian theology, then, was based upon the mythology which preceded it and supplied the mould. So is it with the Hebrew and Christian theology. But here is the difference betwixt them. The mythology remained extant in Egypt, so that the beginnings of the theology could be known and tested, and were known to the mystery teachers, and the origins referred to for the purpose of verification. The commentary which has been partially incorporated with the text of chapter 17 survives to show the development of the theology from mythology and the need of explanations for the Ritual to be understood; and it was these necessary explanations which constituted the gnosis or wisdom of the " mystery teachers of the secret word", whereas the Hebrew and Christian theologies have been accepted minus the necessary knowledge of the origins, the means of applying the comparative method and checking false assumptions. In Christianity the mysteries have been manufactured out of mist, and it has been taken for granted that the mist was impenetrable and never to be seen through, whereas the mysteries of the Ritual can be followed in the two phases of mythology and eschatology. The main difference betwixt the mythos and the eschatology is that the one is represented in the earth of time, the other in the earth of eternity. And if we take the doctrine of a resurrection from the dead, the soul that rose again at first, in mythology, was a soul of the returning light, a soul of life in vegetation, or other of the elemental powers; a soul in external nature. For instance, a soul of life, as source of drink, was apprehended in the element of water, seen also in the plant and figured in the fish. The superhuman type was divinized in Horus. A soul of life, as source of breath, was apprehended in the breeze, and imaged as the panting of a lion. The superhuman type was divinized in Shu. A soul of food was apprehended in the earth, and represented by the goose that laid the egg. The superhuman type was divinized in Seb.

In the Masonic and all other known mysteries, ancient or modern, the initiate has his eyes bandaged so that he may enter the reception room blindfold. This figure, in the Egyptian mysteries, is Horus in the dark, sometimes called the blind Horus, An–ar–ef. In the mythos Horus is the sun in the darkness of Amenta and the depths of the winter solstice. He is the prototype of "blind Orion hungering for the morn", and of Samson "eyeless in Gaza". The character was founded in the mythical representation of natural phenomena, and was afterwards continued in the eschatology. The same type serves in the two categories of phenomena which are here distinguished as the mythical and the eschatological. In the latter the sightless Horus images the human soul in the darkness of death, where it is blind from lack of outer vision. This duality may serve to explain the two–fold rendering of the eyes. According to the hieroglyphic imagery, Horus is without eyes or sightless in one character. He is also portrayed in another as the prince of sight, or of double sight. This, according to the mythos, is a figure of the risen sun and of dawn upon the coffin–lid of Osiris in Amenta. In the eschatology it is Horus, lord of the two eyes, or double vision–that is, of second sight–the seer in spirit with the beatific vision which was attained by him in death. The change from one character to the other is represented in the mysteries by the unbandaging of the initiate's eyes, which are intentionally dazzled by the glory of the lights.The Egyptian Book of the Dead is the one sole record of this two–fold basis of the mysteries.

Enough has now been cited to show the method of the Ritual and the mode in which the eschatology of the Egyptian religion was founded in the mould of the pre–extant mythology. The Book of the Dead is the Egyptian book of life. It is the pre–Christian word of God. This we learn from the account which it gives of itself. It is attributed to Ra as the inspiring holy spirit. Ra was the father in heaven, who has the title of *Huhi*, the eternal, from which we derive the Hebrew name of Ihuh. The word was given by God the father to the ever–coming son as manifestor for the father. This was Horus, who as the coming son is Iu–sa or Iu–su, and, as the prince of peace, Iu–em–hetep. Horus the son is the Word in person. Hence the speaker in the character of Horus says, "I utter his words – the words of Ra – to the men of the present generation, and I repeat his words to him who is deprived of breath" (ch. 38). That is, as Horus, the sayer or logos, who utters the words of Ra the father in heaven to the living on earth, and to the breathless Manes in Amenta when he descends into Hades or the later hell to preach to the spirits in prison. The word or the sayings thus originated with Ra the father in heaven. They were uttered by Horus the son, and when written down in hieroglyphics by the fingers of Taht–Aan for human guidance they supplied a basis for the Book of the Dead. It had been ordained by Ra that his words, such as those that bring about " the resurrection and the glory" (Rit., ch. I), should be written down by the divine scribe Taht–Aan, to make the word truth, and to effect the triumph of Osiris against his adversaries; and it is proclaimed in the opening chapter that this mandate has been obeyed by Taht. The Ritual purports to contain the gnosis of salvation from the second death, together with the ways and means of attaining eternal life, as these were acted in the drama of the Osirian mysteries. Hence the Osiris says that freedom from perdition can be assured by means of this book, in which he trusts and by which he steadfastly abides. The object of the words of power, the magical invocations, the funeral ceremonies, the purgatorial trials, is the resurrection of the mortal to the life which is everlasting. The opening chapter is described as the " words" which bring about the resurrection on the Mount of Glory, and the closing chapters show the deceased upon the summit of attainment. He has joined the lords of eternity in "the circle of Osiris", and in the likeness of his own human self, the very "figure which he had on earth", but changed and glorified (ch.

178). Therefore the most exact and comprehensive title for the Book of the Dead now put together in 186 chapters would be "The Ritual of the Resurrection", The book of the divine words written down by Taht are in the keeping of Horus the son, who is addressed as " him who sees the father". The Manes comes to him with his copy of the writings, by means of which he prevails on his journey through Amenta, like Pilgrim with his roll. He exclaims: "O thou great seer who beholdest his father! O keeper of the books of Taht! Here am I glorified and filled with soul and power, and provided with the writings of Taht", the secrets of which are divine for lightening the darkness of the nether earth (Rit: ch. 94). With these the Manes is accoutred and equipped. The Word of god personified in Horus preceded the written word of god and when the words of power were written down by Taht the scribe of truth, they were assigned to Horus as the logia of the Lord, and preserved as the precious records of him who was the word in person; first the word of power as the founder, then the word in truth or made truth, as the fulfiller. The divine words when written constituted the scriptures, earliest of which are those ascribed to Hermes or Taht, the reputed author of all the sacred writings. And now we find that both the word in person and the written word, together with the doctrine of the word according to the ancient wisdom, are more or less extant and living still in the Egyptian Book of the Dead. The magical words of power when written down by Taht became the nucleus of the Ritual, which is late in comparison with the astronomical mythology and other forms of Sign–language, and belongs mainly to the Osirian religion.

The mystical word of power from the first was female. Apt at Ombos was worshipped as the "the Living Word". The supreme type of this power borne upon the head of Shu is the hinder part of a lioness, her sign of sexual potency. The thigh or khepsh of Apt is also the typical Ur–heka, and it is a symbol of the great magical power. The Ur–heka or magical sign preceded words, and words preceded the writings. Great magical words of power are ascribed to Isis, whose word of power in the human sphere was personified in Horus the child, her word that issued out of silence. This is the word that wvas made flesh in a mortal likeness, the soul derived from blood. Child–Horus, however, manifests in divers phenomena as the Word–of–Power emaned by Isis, in the water, in vegetation, in food, and lastly in the virgin mother's blood. The first Horus was the Word–of–Power, the second is the Word–made–Truth in

Horus, Mat, t–Kheru, by doing it. Horus the Word–of–Power was the founder, who was followed by Horus the Fulfiller. This title does not merely mean the Word of Truth, the True Logos (Celsus), or the True Voice (Plutarch), but denotes the Word–made–Truth or Law by Horus the Victorious, the father's own anointed son, who fulfilled the Word of Power. It is Horus the Word–of–Power personalized as a little child who survives as the miraculous worker two or three years old in the apocryphal gospels. He is credited with doing these infantine marvels as the Word–of–Power in person. He also utters the word of power in performing his amazing miracles.

The magical words were orally communicated in the mysteries from mouth to ear, not written to be read. They were to be gotten by heart. In the Book of the Dead memory is restored to the deceased through the words of power that were stored up in life to be remembered in death. The speaker in chapter 90 says: "O thou who restorest memory in the mouth of the dead through the words of power which they possess, let my mouth be opened through the words of power which I possess". That is, by virtue of the gnosis, memory was restored by the deceased remembering the divine words. Now, Plato taught that a knowledge of past lives in a human pre–existence was restored to persons in this life by means of memory. The origin of the doctrine is undoubtedly Egyptian, but it was made out by a perversion of the original teaching. This restoration of or through memory occurs to the Manes in Amenta after death, and the things remembered appertain to the past life on earth. Plato has misapplied it to the past lives and pre-existence of human beings dwelling on the earth. The words of power were not only spoken. They were likewise represented in the equipment of the mummy, sometimes called its ornaments, such as the word of salvation by the blood of Isis with the red Tet-buckle, the word of durability by the white stone, the word of resurrection by the scarabaeus, the word of eternal life by the cross, called the ankh. These were forms of the magical words expressed in fetish figures.

The Manes in Amenta begins his course where he left off on earth when his mouth was closed in death; it is opened once more for him by Ptah and Tum, and Taht supplies him with the great magical words of power that open every gate. These were written on the roll of papyrus that is carried in his hand by the pilgrim who makes his progress through the nether regions in the subterranean pathway of the sun. The so-called Book of the Dead, then, here quoted as the Ritual for the sake of brevity, is the Egyptian book of life: life now, life hereafter, everlasting life. It was indeed the book of life and salvation, because it contained the things to be done in the life here and hereafter to ensure eternal continuity (Rit., ch. 15, hymn 3). The departing soul when passing away in death, or, as the truer phrase is, when setting into the land of life, clasps and clings to his roll for very life. As the book of life, or word of salvation, it was buried in the coffin with the dead when done with on earth. It showed the way to heaven objectively as well as subjectively, as heaven was mapped out in the astral mythos. The Manes enters Amenta with a papyrus roll in his hand corresponding to the one that was buried in his coffin. This contains the written word of truth, the word of magical power, the word of life. The great question now for him is how far he has made the word of god (Osiris) truth and established it against the powers of evil in his lifetime on the earth. The word that he carries with him was written by Taht–Aan, the scribe of truth. Another word has been written in his lifetime by himself, and the record will meet him in the Hall of Justice on the day of weighing words, when Taht will read the record of the life to see how far it tallies with the written word and how far he has fulfilled the word in truth to earn eternal life. The sense of sin and abhorrence of injustice must have been peculiarly keen when it was taught that every word as well as deed was weighed in the balance of truth on the day of reckoning, called the Judgment Day. The questions confronting the Manes on entering Amenta are whether he has laid sufficient hold of life to live again in death? Has he acquired consistency and strength or truth of character enough to persist in some other more permanent form of personality? Has he sufficient force to incorporate his soul anew and germinate and grow and burst the mummy bandages in the glorified body of the Sahu? Is he a true mummy? Is the backbone sound? Is his heart in the right place? Has he planted for eternity in the seed-field of time? Has he made the word of Osiris, the word that was written in the papyrus roll, truth against his enemies?

The chapters for opening the Tuat, for dealing with the adversary in the nether world, for issuing forth victoriously and thus winning the crown of triumph, for removing displeasure from the heart of the judge, tend to show the ways of attaining the life everlasting by acquiring possession of an eternal soul. The Manes is said to be made safe for the place of rebirth in Annu by means of the books of Taht's divine words, which contain the gnosis or knowledge of the things to be done on earth and in Amenta. The truth is made known by the words of Horus which were written down by Taht in the Ritual, but the fulfilment depends on the Manes making the word truth by doing it. That is the only way of salvation or of safety for the soul, the only mode of becoming a true being who would endure as pure spirit forever. The Egyptians had no vicarious atonement, no imputed righteousness, no second–hand salvation. No initiate in the Osirian mysteries could possibly have rested his hope of reaching heaven on the Galilean line to glory. His was the more crucial way of Amenta, which the Manes had to tread with the guidance of the word, that step by step and act by act he must himself make true. It is said in the rubrical directions of chapter 72 that the Manes who knew it on earth and had it written on his coffin will be able to go in and out by day under any form he chooses in which he can penetrate his dwelling–place and also make his way to the Aarru fields of peace and plenty, where he will be flourishing for ever even as he was on earth (Rit., 72, 9, II). I f chapter 91 is known, the Manes takes the form of a fully–equipped spirit (a Khu) in the nether world, and is not imprisoned at any door in Amenta either going in or coming out. (Chapter 92) is the one that opens the tomb to the soul and to the shade of a person, that he may come forth to day and have the mastery over his feet. The book of giving sustenance to the spirit of the deceased in the under-world delivers the person from all evil things (Rit., 148). There was another book wherewith the spirits acquired strength by knowing the names of the gods of the southern sky and of the northern sky (chs. 141–3). The Ritual was pre-eminently a book of knowledge or of wisdom, because it contained the gnosis of the mysteries. Knowledge was all-important. The Manes make their passage through Amenta by means of what they know. Deceased in one of his supplications says: "O thou ship of the garden Aarru, let me be conveyed to that bread of thy canal, as my father the great one who advanceth in the divine ship, *because I know thee*" (ch. 106, Renouf). He knew because, as we see by (ch. 99,) he had learned the names of every part of the bark in which the spirits sailed. Knowledge was power, knowledge was the gnosis, and the gnosis was the science of the mystery teachers and the masters of Sign-language. Ignorance was most dire and deadly. How could one travel in the next world any more than in this without knowing the way? The way in Amenta was indicated topographically very much in keeping with the ways in Egypt, chief of which was the water-way of the great river. Directions, names, and passwords were furnished in writing, to be placed with the mummy of the deceased. Better still, if these instructions and divine teachings were learned by heart, had been enacted and the word made truth in the life, then the Book of the Dead if life became the book of life in death. The word was given that it might be made truth by doing it as the means of learning the way by knowing the word. The way of life in three worlds, those of earth, Amenta, and heaven, was by knowing the word of god and making it true in defiance of all the powers of evil. According to this earlier Bible, death came into the world by ignorance, not by knowledge, as in the Christian travesty of the Egyptian teaching. As Hermes says: "The wickedness of a soul is ignorance. The virtue of a soul is knowledge" (*Divine Pymander,* B. iv., 27, 28).There was no life for the soul except in knowing, and no salvation but in doing. the truth. The human soul of Neferuben in the picture is the wise or instructed soul, one of the Khu–Akaru : he is a master of the gnosis, a knower or knowing soul, and therefore not to be caught like an ignorant fish in the net. Knowledge is of the first importance. In all his journeyings and difficulties it is necessary for the deceased to *know*. It is by knowledge that he is lighted to find his way in the dark. Knowledge is his lamp of light and his compass; to possess knowledge is to be master of divine powers and magical words. Ignorance would leave him a prey to all sorts of liers in wait and cunning enemies. He triumphs continually through his knowledge of the way, like a traveller with his chart and previous acquaintanceship with the local language; hence the need of the gnosis and of initiation in the mysteries. Those who knew the real name of the god were in possession of the word that represented power over the divinity, therefore the word of power that would be efficacious if employed. Instead of calling on the name of god in prayer, they made use of the name as the word of god. And as these words and mysteries of magic were contained in the writings, it was necessary to know the writings in which the gnosis was religiously preserved to be in possession of the words of power. Hence the phrases of great magical efficacy in the Ritual are called "the words that compel". They compel the favourable action of the super–human power to which appeal is made. To *make* magic was to *act* the appeal in a language of signs which, like the words, were also intended to compel, and to act thus magically was a mode of compelling, forcing, and binding the superhuman powers. Magic was also a mode of covenanting with the power apprehended in the elements. The *quid pro quo* being blood, this was a most primitive form of blood–covenant. Giving blood for food was giving life for the means of living.

The Ritual opens with a resurrection, but this is the resurrection in the earth of Amenta, not in the heaven of eternity. It is the resurrection of a body–soul emerging in the similitude of the moon–god from the dark of death. The first words of the Ritual are, "O Bull of Amenta [Osiris], it is Taht, the everlasting king, who is here!". He has come as one of the powers that fight to secure the triumph of Osiris over all his adversaries. After the life on earth there was a resurrection in Amenta, the earth of eternity, for the human soul evolved on earth. I t was there that the claim to the resurrection in spirit and to life eternal in heaven had to be made good and established by long and painful experiences and many kinds of purgatorial purification, by which the soul was perfected eventually as an ever–living spirit. The word of promise had to be performed and made truth indeed, for the Ma–Kheru of immortality to be earned and endless continuity of life assured. Everyone who died was in possession of a body–soul that passed into Amenta to become an Osiris or an image of the god in matter, although it was not every one who was reborn or regenerated in the likeness of Ra, to attain the

Horushood, which was portrayed as the *hood* of the divine hawk. Emergence in Amenta was the coming forth of the human soul from the coffin and from the gloom of the grave in some form of personality such as is depicted in the Shade, or the Ba, a bird of soul with the human head, which shows that a human soul is signified. Osiris the god of Amenta in a mummy form is thus addressed by the Osiris N. or Manes: "O breathless one, let me live and be saved after death" (ch. 41). This is addressed to Osiris who lives eternally. Though lying as a mummy in Amenta, breathless and without motion, he will be self–resuscitated to rise again. Salvation is renewal for another life; to be saved is not to suffer the second death, not to die a second time. According to Egyptian thought, the saved are the living and the twice dead are the damned. Life after death is salvation of the soul, and those not saved are those who die the second death – a fate that could not be escaped by any false belief in the merits of Horus or the efficacy of the atoning blood. There was no heaven to be secured for them by proxy.

The Ritual is not a book of beautiful sentiments, like the poetic literature of later times. It is a record of the things done by the *dramatis personae* in the Kamite mysteries. But now and again the beauty of feeling breaks out ineffably upon the face of it, as in the chapter by which the deceased prevails over his adversaries, the powers of darkness, and comes forth to the day, saying, "O thou who shinest forth from the moon, thou that givest light from the moon, let me come forth at large amid thy train, and be revealed as one of those in glory. Let the Tuat be opened for me. Here am I". The speaker is in Amenta as a mummy soul appealing to the father of lights and lord of spirits that he may come forth in the character of Horus divinized to delight the soul of his poor mother. He wishes to capitalize the desires of those who "make salutations" to the gods on his behalf. These in modern parlance would be the prayers of the priests and congregation (ch. 3) for his welfare and safety in the future life, otherwise for his salvation. In the chapter by which one cometh forth to day he pleads: "Let me have possession of all things soever which were offered ritualistically for me in the nether world. Let me have possession of the table of offerings which was heapt for me on earth – the solicitations which were uttered for me, *that he may feed upon the bread of Seb*,' or the food of earth. Let me have possession of my funeral meals", the meals offered on earth for the dead in the funerary chamber (ch.68).

The chief object of the deceased on entering Amenta is the mode and means of getting out again as soon as possible upon the other side. His one all-absorbing interest is the resurrection to eternal life. He says, "Let me reach the land of ages, let me gain the land of eternity, for thou, my Lord, hast destined them for me" (ch. 13).Osiris or *the* Osiris passed into Amenta as the lord of transformations. Various changes of shape were necessitated by the various modes of progression. As a beetle or a serpent he passed through solid earth, as a crocodile through the water, as a hawk through the air. As a jackal or a cat he saw in the dark; as an ibis he was the knowing one, or "he of the nose". Thus he was the master of transformations, the magician of the later folk-tales, who could change his shape at will. Taht is termed the great magician as the lord of transformations in the moon. Thus the deceased in assuming the type of Taht becomes a master of transformation or the magician whose transformations had also been made on earth by the transformers in trance who pointed the way to transformation in death. When Teta comes to consciousness on rising again in Amenta he is said to have broken his sleep for ever which was in the dwelling of Seb – that is, on the earth. He has now received his Sahu or investiture of the glorious body.

Before the mortal Manes could attain the ultimate state of spirit in the image of Horus the immortal, he must be put together part by part as was Osiris, the dismembered god. He is divinized in the likeness of various divinities, all of whom had been included as powers in the person of the one true god, Neb–er–ter, the lord entire. Every member and part of the Manes in Amenta has to be fashioned afresh in a new creation. The new heart is said to be shaped by certain gods in the nether world, according to the deeds done in the body whilst the person was living on the earth. He assumes the glorified body that is formed feature by feature and limb after limb in the likeness of the gods until there is no part of the Manes that remains undivinized. He is given the hair of Nu, or heaven, the eyes of Hathor, ears of Apuat, nose of Khenti–Kâs, lips of Anup, teeth of Serk, neck of Isis, hands of the mighty lord of Tat tu, shoulders of Neith, back of Sut, phallus of Osiris, legs and thighs of Nut, feet of Ptah, with nails and bones of the living Uraei, until there is not a limb of him that is without a god. There is no possibility of coming back to earth for a new body or for a re–entry into the old mummy. As the Manes says, his "soul is not bound to his old body at the gates of Amenta" (ch. 26, 6). Chapter 89 is designated the chapter by which the soul is united to the body. This, however, does not mean the dead body on earth, but the *format* or bodily type of the mummy in Amenta.

"Here I come", says the speaker, that "I may overthrow mine adversaries upon the earth, *though my dead body be buried*" (ch. 86, Renouf). "Let me come forth to day, and walk upon my own legs. Let me have the feet of the glorified" (ch. 86). At this stage he exclaims, "I am a soul, and my soul is divine. It is the eternal force". In chapters 21 and 22 the Manes asks for his mouth, that he may speak with it. Having his mouth restored, he asks that it may be opened by Ptah, and that Taht may loosen the fetters or muzzles of Sut, the power of darkness (ch. 23). In short,' that he may recover the faculty of speech. In the process of transforming and being renewed as the new man, the second Atum, he says, "I am Khepera, the self–produced upon his mother's thigh". Khepera is the beetle–type of the sun that is portrayed in pictures of the goddess Nut proceeding from the mother's khepsh. The name of the beetle signifies becoming and evolving, hence it is a type of the becomer in making his transformation. The mouth being given, words of power are brought to him, he also gathers them from every quarter. Then he remembers his name. Next the new heart is given to him. His jaws are parted, his eyes are opened. Power is given to his arms and vigour to his legs. He is in possession of his heart, his mouth, his eyes, his limbs, and his speech. He is now a new man reincorporated in the body of a Sahu, with a soul that is no longer bound to the Khat or dead mummy at the gates of Amenta (ch. 26). He looks forward to being fed upon the food of Osiris in Aarru, on the eastern side of the mead of amaranthine flowers.

In one phase of the drama the deceased is put together bone by bone in correspondence to the backbone of Osiris. The backbone was an emblem of sustaining power, and this reconstruction of deceased is in the likeness of the mutilated god. The speaker at this point says, "The four fastenings of the hinder part of my head are made firm". He does not fall at the block. There are of course seven cervical vertebrae in the backbone altogether, but three of these are peculiar, " the atlas which supports the head, the axis upon which the head turns, and the *vertebrae prominens*, with its long spiral process" (ch. 30, Renouf).No doubt the Osiris was rebuilt upon this model, and the four joints were fundamental, they constituted a four–fold foundation. In another passage the Osiris is apparently perfected "upon the square", as in the Masonic mysteries. It is the chapter by which one assumes the form of Ptah, the great architect of the universe. The speaker says, "He is four times the arm's length of Ra, four times the width of the world" (Rit., ch. 82, Renouf), which is a mode of describing the four quarters or four sides of the earth, as represented by the Egyptians. There were seven primary powers in the mythical and astronomical phases, six of whom are represented by zootypes, and the seventh is imaged in the likeness of a man. This is repeated in the eschatology, where the highest soul of seven is the Ka–eidolon with a human face and figure as the final type of spirit which was human on the earth and is to be eternal in the heavens. The Manes who is being reconstituted says, "The [seven] Uraeus divinities *are my body*. ...My image is eternal" (ch. 85), as it would be when the seven souls were amalgamated into one that was imaged by the divine Ka. The seven Uraeus divinities represented the seven souls of life that were anterior to the one enduring soul. In the chapter of propitiating one's own Ka the Manes says, "Hail to thee, my Ka! May I come to thee and be glorified and made manifest and *ensouled?*" (ch. 103)–that is, in attaining the highest of the souls, the unifying one. These souls may be conceived as seven ascending types of personality. The first is figured as the shade, the dark soul or shade of the Inoits, the Greenlanders, and other aboriginal races, which is portrayed personally in the Ritual lying darkly on the ground. The shade was primary, because of its being, as it were, a shadow of the old body projected on the ground in the new life. It is portrayed as a black figure stretched out in Amenta. In this way the earth shadow of the body in life served as the *type* of a soul that passed out of the body in death. This may explain the intimate relationship of the shade to the physical mummy, which it is sometimes said to cling to and remain with in the tomb, and to draw sustenance from the corpse so long as it exists. Thus the shade that draws life from the dead body becomes the mythical prototype of the vampire and the legendary ghoul. It may be difficult to determine exactly what the Egyptians understood by the khabit or shade in its genesis as a soul, but the Inoit or Aleutians describe it as "a vapour emanating from the blood" and here is wisdom for those who comprehend it. The earliest human soul, derived from the mother when the blood was looked upon as the life, was a soul of blood, and the Inoit description answers perfectly to the shade in the Egyptian Amenta. Amongst the most primitive races the typical basis of a future personality is the shade. The Aleutians say the soul at its departure divides into the shade and the spirit. The first dwells in the tomb, the other ascends to the firmament. These, wherever met with, are equivalent to the twin-souls of Sut the dark one, and Horus the soul of light. For we reckon the Egyptian seven to be earliest and old enough to account for and explain the rest which are to be found dispersed about the world. The soul as shade or shadow is known to the Macusi Indians as the "man in the eyes" who "does not die". This is another form of the shadow that was not cast upon the ground. Dr. Birch drew attention to the fact that whilst the deceased has but one Ba, one Sahu, and one Ka, he has two shades, his Khabti being in the plural (*Trans. Society of Bib. Arch.*, volume viii., page 391). These two correspond to the dark and light shades of the aborigines. They also conform to the two souls of darkness and light that were imaged by the black vulture and the golden hawk of Sut and Horus, the first two of the total septenary of powers or souls. The shade, however, is but one–seventh of the series. The other self when perfected consists of seven amalgamated souls. Some of the Manes in Amenta do not get beyond the state of the shade or Khabit; they are arrested in this condition of mummied immobility. They do not acquire the new heart or soul of breath; they remain in the egg unhatched, and do not become the Ba–soul or the glorified Khu. These are the souls that are said to be eaten by certain of the gods or infernal powers. "Eater of the shades" is the title of the fourth of the forty–two executioners (ch. 125). The tenth of the mystical abodes in Amenta is the place of the monstrous arms that capture and carry away the Manes who have not attained a condition beyond that of the shade or empty shell. The "shells" of the theosophists may be met with in the Ritual. The Manes who is fortified with his divine soul can pass this place in safety. He says, "Let no one take possession of my shade [let no one take possession of my shell or envelope]. I am the divine hawk". He has issued from the shell of the egg and been established beyond the status of the shade as a Ba–soul. With this may be compared the superstition that in eating eggs one should always break up the empty shell, lest it should be made evil use of by the witches. There are wretched shades condemned to immobility in the fifth of the mystical abodes. They suffer their final arrest in that place and position, and are then devoured by the giants who live as eaters of the shades. These monsters are described as having thigh–bones seven cubits long (ch. 149,18,19). No mere shade has power enough to pass by these personifications of devouring might; they are the ogres of legendary lore. who may be found at home with the ghoul and the vampire in the dark caverns of the Egyptian under world. These were the dead whose development in spirit world was arrested at the status of the shade, and who were supposed to seek the life they lacked by haunting and preying upon human souls, particularly on the soul of blood. In its next stage the soul is called a Ba, and is represented as a hawk with a human head, to show that the nature of the soul is human still. This is more than a soul of shade, but it was not imagined nor believed that the human soul as such inhabited the body of a bird. In one of the hells the shades are seen burning, but these were able to resist the fire, and it is consequently said, "The shades live; *they have raised their powers*". They are raised in status by assimilating higher powers.

Following his taking possession of the soul of shade and the soul of light the Osiris is given a new heart, his whole or two–fold heart. With some of the primitive folk, as with the Basutos, it is the heart that goes out in death as the soul that never dies. Bobadilla a learned from the Indians of Nicaragua that there are two different hearts; that one of these went away with the deceased in death, and that it was the heart that went away which "made them live" hereafter. This other breathing heart, the basis of the future being, is one with the Egyptian heart by which the reconstituted person lives again. The heart that was weighed in the Hall of Judgment could not have been the organ of life on earth. This was a second heart, the heart of another life. The Manes makes appeal for this heart not to bear evidence against him in presence of the god who is at the balance (chs. 30A and 30B). The second is the heart that was fashioned anew according to the life lived in the body. It is said to be the heart of the great god Tehuti, who personated intelligence. Therefore it would seem to typify the soul of intelligence. Hence it is said to be young and keen of insight among the gods, or among the seven souls. The physical representation comes first, but it is said in the text of Panchemisis, "The conscience or heart (Ab) of a man is his own god" or divine judge. The new heart represents rebirth, and is therefore called the mother (ch. 30A); and when the deceased recovers the basis of future being in his whole heart he says, although he is buried in the deep, deep grave, and bowed down to the region of annihilation, he is glorified (even) there (ch. 30A, Renouf).

Now if we take the shade to image a soul of blood, the Ba–hawk to image a soul of light, and the hati–heart to represent a soul of breath, we can perceive a *raison d' être* for the offering of blood, of lights, and of incense as sacrifices to the Manes in three different phases or states. Blood was generally offered to the shades, as we see in survival among the Greeks and Romans. The shade was in the first stage of the past existence, and most needing in Amenta the blood which was the life on earth and held to be of first necessity for the revivifying of the dead as Manes or shades. The Sekhem was one of the souls or powers. It is difficult to identify this with a type and place in the seven. *Pro tem* we call it fourth of the series. It is more important to know what force it represents. The name is derived from the word khem, for potency. Khem in physics signifies erectile power. The man of thirty years as typical adult is khemt. Sekhem denotes having the power or potency of the erectile force. In the eschatological phase it is the reproducing, formative power of Khem, or Amsu, to re–erect, the power of erection being applied to the spirit in fashioning and vitalizing the new and glorious body for the future resurrection *from* Amenta. The Khu is a soul in which the person has attained the status of the pure in spirit called the glorified, represented in the likeness of a beautiful white bird; the Ka is a type of eternal duration in which the seven–fold personality is unified at last for permanent or everlasting life.

It is the Khu that is thus addressed in the tomb as the glorified one: "Thou shalt not be imprisoned by those who are attached to the person of Osiris [that is, the mummy], and who have custody of souls and spirits, and who shut up the shades of the dead. It is heaven only that shall hold thee". (Rit. ch., 92.) The shade of itself could never leave the tomb. For this reason it was commonly held that the shade remained with the corpse or mummy on the earth. But here the tomb, the mummy, and the shade are not on earth; they are in Amenta. Without the Ba–soul, the shade remains unvivified. Without the Sekhem, it lacks essential form or power of re–arising. Without the Khu–spirit the person does not ascend from the sepulchre or prison–house of the nether world. But when this has been attained the deceased is glorified. If chapter 91 is known, "he taketh the form of a fully–equipped Khu [spirit] in the nether world, and does not suffer imprisonment at any door in Amenta, either in coming in or going out" (Renouf, ch. 91). It is only when the Manes is invested as a Khu that he ascends to the father as a son of god. So we gather from the following words addressed to Horus by the person who is now a Khu: "O mighty one, who seest thy father, and who hast charge of the books of Taht, here am I. I come, and am glorified and filled with soul and power, and am provided with the scriptures of Taht", his copy of the book of life, his light in the darkness of Amenta. He now ascends to Ra his father, who is in the bark, and exclaims again and again, "I am a powerful Khu; let thy soundness be my soundness" (Renouf, ch. 105). When the deceased has been made perfect as a Khu, he is free to enter the great house of seven halls (ch. 145). Likewise the "house of him who is upon the hill", and who is "ruler in the divine hall". The great house is the heaven of Osiris based upon the thirty–six gates or duo–decans of the zodiac. The other is the house of Anup at the summit of the mount in Annu. "Behold me", he exclaims; "behold me, I am come to you, and have *carried off and put together my forms*", or constituent parts of the permanent soul, which were seven altogether. These are: (1) The Khabit or dark shade; (2) the Ba or light shade; (3) the breathing heart; (4) the Sekhem; (5) the Sahu; (6) the Khu; (7) the Ka. When the Manes has become a Khu, the Ka is still a typical ideal ahead of him; so far ahead or aloof that he propitiates it with offerings. In fact, he presents himself as the sacrificial victim that would die to attain conjunction with his Ka, his image of eternal duration, his type of totality, in which the seven souls were permanently unified in one at last. The Ka has been called the double of the dead, as if it simply represented the *Doppel–ganger*. But it is not merely a phantom of the living or personal image of the departed. It serves also for the apparition or *revenant* ; it is a type rather than a portrait. It is a type that was pre–natal. It images a soul which came into existence with the child, a soul which is food and sustenance to the body all through life, a soul of existence here and of duration for the life hereafter. Hence it is absorbed at last in the perfected personality. It is depicted in the Temple of Luxor, where the birth of Amen–hetep III. is portrayed as coming from the hand of god. The Ka of the royal infant is shown in the pictures being formed by Khnum the moulder on the potter's wheel. It is in attendance on the person all life through, as the genius or guardian angel, and the fulfilment of the personality is effected by a final reunion with the Ka. As already shown, when divine honours were paid to the Pharaoh the offerings were made to his Ka, not to his mortal self. Thus the Manes in Amenta makes an offering of incense to purify himself in propitiation of his Ka (ch. 105). There is a chapter of "providing food for the Ka". Also the mortuary meal was eaten in the chamber of the Ka, the resurrection chamber of the sepulchre. Food was offered to the Ka–eidôlon as the representative of the departed, instead of directly to the spirits of the ancestors. It was set up there as receiver–general of the offerings. Also the food was presented to it as a type of the divine food which sustained the human soul. Thus, when the divine sustenance is offered by the god or goddess to the soul of the mortal on the earth, or to the Manes in Amenta, it is presented by the giver to the Ka. Certain priests were appointed to be ministers to the Ka, and these made the offerings to the Ka of the deceased on behalf of the living relatives. This is because the Ka was the type of personality, seventh of the seven souls attained as the highest in which the others were to be included and absorbed. In the vignettes to chapter 25 of the Ritual (Naville, *Todt.*, *Kap.*, 25, vol. i., p. 36) the deceased is shown his Ka, which is with him in the passage of Amenta, not left behind him in the tomb, that he may not forget himself (as we might say), or, as he says, that he may not suffer loss of identity by *forgetting his name.* Showing the Ka to him enables the Manes to recall his name in the great house, and especially in the crucible of the house of flame. When the deceased is far advanced on his journey through Amenta, his Ka is still accompanying him, and it is described as being the food of his life in spirit world, even as it had been his spiritual food in the human life. "Thou art come, Osiris; thy Ka is with thee. Thou feedest thyself under thy name of Ka" (128,6). When the Osiris has passed from the state of a shade to the stage of the Ka, he will become what the Ritual designates a fully equipped Manes who has completed his investiture. As a Sahu he was reincorporated in a spiritual body. As a Khu he was invested with a robe of glory. As a sacred hawk with the head of a Bennu he was endowed with the soul of Horus (ch. 78). It was here he exclaimed "Behold me; I am come to you [the gods and the glorified], and have carried off my forms and united them". But in chapter 92 he was anxiously looking forward to the day of reckoning, when he said, "Let the way be open to my soul and my shade, that I may see the great god within his sanctuary on the day of the soul's reckoning", "when all hearts and words are weighed". He is not yet one of the spirits made perfect, being neither judged nor justified. He has to pass his last examination, and is now approaching the great hall of judgment for his trial. He says, "I am come that I may secure my suit in Abydos", the mythical re:–birthplace of Osiris. This is the final trial of the long series through which he has hitherto. successfully passed (Rit, ch. II 7, Renouf). He has now arrived at the judgment hall. It has been asserted that the deeds which the deceased had done here on earth in no wise influenced the fate that awaited the man after death (Maspero, *Egyptian Archaeology*. Eng. tr., p. 149). But how so, when the new heart which was given to the deceased in Amenta, where he or she was reconstituted, is said to be *fashioned in accordance with what he has done in his human life?* And the speaker pleads that his new heart may *not be fashioned according to all the evil things that may be said against him* (Rit., ch. 27). He is anxious that the ministrants of Osiris in the Neter-Kar, "who deal with a man *according to the course of his life*", may not give a bad odour to his name (ch. 3OB). And again he pleads,"Let me be glorified through my attributes; let me be estimated according to my merits" (ch.72). It is plainly apparent that the future fate of the soul was dependent on the deeds that were done in the body, and the character of the deceased was accreted according to his conduct in the life on earth.

The jury sitting in the judgment hall consisted of forty-two masters of truth. Their duty was to discover the truth with fierce interrogation and the instinct of sleuth-hounds on their track. Was this Manes a true man? Had he lived a true life? Was he true at heart when this was tested in the scales? His viscera were present for inspection, and these keen scrutinizers in their animal-headed forms were very terrible, not only in visage, for they had a vested interest in securing a verdict of guilty against the Manes, inasmuch as the viscera of the condemned were flung to them as perquisites and prey, therefore they searched with the zeal of hunger for the evidence of evil living that might be found written on this record of the inner man. Piecemeal the Manes were examined, to be passed if true, to be sent back if not, in the shape of swine or goats or other typhonian animals, and driven down into the fiery lake of outer darkness where Baba the devourer of hearts, the Egyptian "raw–head–and–bloody–bones", was lying in wait for them. The highest verdict rendered by the great judge in this most awful Judgment Hall was a testimony to the truth and purity of character established for the Manes on evidence that was unimpeachable. At this *post–mortem* the sins done in the body through violating the law of nature were probed for most profoundly. Not only was the deceased present in spirit to be judged at the dread tribunal, the book of the body was opened and its record read. The vital organs, such as the heart, liver, and lungs, were brought into judgment as witnesses to the life lived on earth. Any part too vitiated for the rottenness to be cut off or scraped away was condemned and flung as offal to the powers who are called the eaters of filth, the devourers of hearts, and drinkers of the blood of the wicked. And if the heart, for example, should be condemned to be devoured because very bad, the individual could not be reconstructed for a future life.

In order that the Osiris may pass the Great Assize as one of the justified, he must have made the word of Osiris truth on earth against his enemies. He must have lived a righteous life and been just, truthful, merciful, charitable, humane. In coming to the Hall of Judgment or Justice to look on the divine countenance and be cleansed from all the sins he may have committed he says, "I have come to thee, O my Lord. I know thee. Lord of Righteousness is thy name. I bring to thee right. I have put a stop to wrong". His plea is that he has done his best to fulfil the character of Horus–Makheru. Some of his pleas are very touching. "He has not exacted from the labourer, as the first–fruits of each day, more work than was justly due to him. He has not snatched the milk from the mouths of babes and sucklings. He has not been a land–grabber. He has not dammed the running water. He has caused no famine, no weeping, no suffering to men, and has not been a robber of food. He has not tampered with the tongue of the balance, nor been fraudulent, mean, or sordid of soul. There is a goodly list of pre–Christian virtues besides all the theoretical Christian ones. Amongst others, he says, "I have propitiated the god with that which he'loveth". This was especially by the offering of *Maat*, viz., justice, truth, and righteousness. "I have given bread to the hungry, water to the thirsty, clothes to the naked, and a boat to the shipwrecked" (ch. 125). Yet we have been told that charity and mercy were totally unknown to the pagan world. He asks the forty–two assessors for the great judge not to go against him, for he did the right thing in Tamerit, the land of Egypt. His heart is weighed in the scales of justice. He passes pure, as one of those who are welcomed by Horus for his own faithful followers, the blessed of his father, to whom it is said, "Come, come in peace". Horus the intercessor, advocate, or paraclete, now takes him by the hand and leads him into the presence of Osiris in the sanctuary. The Manes in the Judgment Hall is black–haired, as seen in the pictures of Ani (Papyrus of Ani, pl. 4). But when he kneels before Osiris on the throne his hair is white. He has passed as one of the purified and is on his way to join the ranks of the just spirits made perfect, who are called the glorified. The attendants say to him, "We put an end to thy ills and we remove that which is disorderly in thee through thy being smitten to the earth" in death. These were the ills of mortality from which he has now been freed in spirit. Here occurs the resurrection of the Osiris in the person of Horus, and it is said, "Ha, Osiris! thou hast come, and thy Ka with thee, which uniteth with thee in thy name of Ka–hetep" (ch. 128). An ordinary rendering of "Ka–hetep" would be "image of peace" = type of attainment; but as the word hetep or hepti also means number seven, that coincides with the Ka being an image of the septenary of souls, complete at last to be unified in the hawk–headed Horus.

In the book or papyrus–roll for invoking the gods of the Kerti, or boundaries, we find the speaker has now reached the limit of Amenta. He says, "I am the soul of Osiris, and rest in him" (ch. 127). He is hailed as one who has attained his Ka and received his insignia of the resurrection. It is now said to the Osiris, "Ha, Osiris! thou hast received thy sceptre, thy pedestal, and the flight of stairs beneath thee" (Rit., ch. 128). The sceptre was the hare–headed symbol of the resurrection first carried by Ptah the opener. The pedestal is the papyrus of Horus, and the stairs denote the means of ascent from Amenta to the summit of the Mount of Glory. He is now prepared and empowered to enter the bark of Ra which voyages from east to west by day and from west to east by night. Before entering the bark the Osiris has attained to everyone of his stations in Amenta previously to sailing for the circumpolar paradise upon the stellar Mount of Glory.

Chapter 130 is the book by which the soul is made to live for ever on the day of entering the bark of Ra, which means that it contains the gnosis of the subject. It was made for the birthday or re–birthday of Osiris. Osiris is re–born in Horus as the type of an eternal soul. Hence the speaker says, in this character, "I am coffined in an ark like Horus, to whom his cradle [or nest of reeds] is brought". He is reborn as Horus on his papyrus, an earlier figure on the water than the bark of Ra. He prays, "Let not the Osiris be shipwrecked on the great voyage; keep the steering tackle free from misadventure". When he entered Amenta the deceased in Osiris bore the likeness of the god in mummy form. Before he comes forth from the lower Aarru garden he can say, at the end of certain transformations in type and personality, "I am the soul of Osiris, and I rest in him" (ch. 127). This is in the character of Horus. "I am Horus on this auspicious day" at the "beautiful coming forth from Amenta". He has reached the boundary, and now invokes the god who is in his solar disk, otherwise in the bark of Ra. He died in Osiris to live again in Horus, son of god, or in his likeness. Chapters 141 and 142 begin the book of making the Osiris perfect. And this, as the Ritual shows, was in the likeness of Horus the beloved sole-begotten son of Ra, the god in spirit. Now, when the Manes had included his Ka in the name of Ka–hetep (Rit., ch. 128) it is said to the deceased (in the Pyramid texts, Teta, 284, Pepi 1.,34), "Horus hath brought to pass that *his* ka, which is in thee, should unite with thee in thy name of Ka–hetep", which shows the Ka within him was the image of Horus divinized. This corroborates the suggestion that the ka–type was derived from Ka (later Sa) the son of Atum–Ra, who was earlier than Horus as the son of Osiris. Thus the divine sonship of humanity which was personified in Horus, or Iu, or Sa, was also typified in the ka–image of a higher spiritual self; and when the Manes had attained the status of a spirit perfected it was in the form of the divine son who was the express image of the father god. He was Horus the beloved, in all reality, through perfecting the ideal type in his own personality.

He now enters the divine presence of Osiris–Ra to relate what he has done in the characters of human Horus, Har–Tema, and Har–Makheru on behalf of his father which constitutes him the veritable son of god. When the Manes had attained the solar bark he has put on "the divine body of Ra" and is hailed by the ministrants with cries of welcome and acclamations from the Mount of Glory (ch. 133). In travelling through the under–world he had passed from the western horizon of earth to the east of heaven, where he joins the solar boat to voyage the celestial waters. There is a change of boat for the night. Hence the speaker says he is "coming in the two barks of the lord of Sau" (ch. 136B, Renouf). There may be some difficulty about the exact position of the chapter numbered 110 in the Ritual, but there is no difficulty in identifying the fields of peace upon the summit of Mount Hetep as the lower paradise of two, which was the land of promise attainable in Amenta. This was the sub–terrestrial or earthly paradise of the legends. When the Manes comes to these elysian fields he is still in the earth of eternity, and has to prove himself an equal as a worker with the mighty Khus (Khuti), who are nine cubits high, in cultivating his allotment of arable land. The arrival at Mount Hetep in this lower paradise or heaven of the solar mythos precedes the entrance to the Judgment Hall which is in the domain of the Osiris below, and the voyage from east to west in the Matit and the Sektit bark of the sun, therefore it is not in the ultimate heaven or the upper paradise of eternity upon Mount Hetep. We see from the Pyramid texts (Pepi I., lines 192, 169, 182, Maspero, *Les Inscripions. des Pyramides de Sakkarah*) that there were two stages of ascent to the upper paradise, that were represented by two ladders : one is the ladder of Sut, as the ascent from the land of darkness, the other is the ladder of Horus, reaching to the land of light. King Pepi salutes the two: "Homage to thee, O ladder of Sut. Set thyself up, O ladder of God. Set thyself up, O ladder of Sut. Set thyself up, O ladder of Horus, whereby Osiris appeared in heaven when he wrought protection for Ra. "Pepi likewise enters heaven in his name of the ladder (*Budge, Book of the Dead, Intro.*, pp. 117, 118). The Manes also says, in ch. 149, "I raise my ladder up to the sky, that I may behold the gods".

But, having traced the reconstruction of the deceased for a future life, we now return, to follow him once more from the entrance to Amenta on his journey through the under–world. His mortal personality having been made a permanent as possible in the mummy left on earth, the Manes rising in Amenta now sets out to attain the personality that is to last for ever. He pleads with all his dumbness that his mouth may be opened, or, in other words, that his memory, which he has lost awhile, may be given back to him, so that he may utter the words of power (chs. 21–23) with which he is equipped. The ceremony of opening the mouth after the silence of death was one of the profoundest secrets. The great type of power by means of which the mouth is opened was the leg of the hippopotamus goddess, the symbol of her mightiness as *primum mobile* in the Great Bear having been adopted for this purpose in the eschatology. The ceremony was performed at the tomb as well as in Amenta by the opener Ptah as a mystery of the resurrection. And amongst the many other survivals this rite of "opening the mouth" is still performed in Rome. It was announced in a daily paper not long since (the *Mail,* August 8th, 1903) that after the death of Pope Leo XIII. and the coronation of Pius X. "a Consistory would be held to close and open the lips of the cardinals newly created", or newly born into the purple. The Osiris also prays that when his mouth is opened Taht may come to him equipped with the words of power. So soon as the mouth of the Manes is freed from the fetters of dumbness and darkness (or muzzles of Sut) and restored to him, he collects the words of power from all quarters more persistently than any sleuth–hound and more swiftly than the flash of light (chs. 23, 24, Renouf). These words of power are magical in their effect. They paralyze all opposition. They open every door. The power is at once applied. The speaker says, "Back, in retreat ! Back, crocodile Sui! Come not against me, who live by the words of power! " (ch. 31). This is spoken to the crocodiles or dragons who come to rob the Manes and carry off the words of power that protect the deceased in death. The magical mode of employing the words of power in the mysteries of Taht is by the deceased being assimilated to the character and assuming the superhuman type as a means of protection against the powers of evil. The speaker in the Ritual does not mistake himself for the deity. He is the deity *pro tem.* in acted Sign–language, and by such means is master of the magical power. It is the god who is the power, and the magician employs the words and signs which express that power; but instead of praying to the god he makes use of the divine words attributed to the god, and personates the god as Horus or Ra, Taht or Osiris, in character. He puts on the mask of a crocodile, an ibis, a lion, or other zootype of the primary powers, and says to his adversaries: I am the crocodile (= Sebek), or, I am the lion (= Atum), or, I am Ra, the sun, protecting himself with the Uraeus serpent, and consequently no evil thing can overthrow me (ch. 32). Repeating ch. 42 was a magical way of escaping from the slaughter which was wrought in Suten–Khen, and the mode of magic was for the deceased in his re–birth to become or to be assimilated to the divine child in his rebirth. He tells the serpent Abur that he is the divine babe, the mighty one. Not a limb of him is without a god. He is not to be grasped by arms or seized by hands. "Not men or gods, the glorified ones or the damned; not generations past, present, or to come, can inflict any injury on him who cometh forth and proceedeth as the eternal child, the everlasting one" (Rit., ch. 42), or as Horus, the son of Isis. These divine characters are assumed by the Manes when he commands his enemies to do his bidding. According to the magical prescriptions, in fighting the devil, or the evil Apap, a figure of the monster was to be moulded in wax with the name inscribed upon it in green (Budge, *Proceedings Soc. of Arch.*, 1866, po 21). This was to be spat upon many times, spurned with the foot, and then flung into the fire, as a magical mode of casting out the devil. When the Apap reptile is first encountered and addressed in the Ritual it is said, "O one of wax! who takest captive and seizest with violence and livest upon those who are motionless, let me not become motionless before thee" (Rit., ch. 7). This is because the presence of the devouring monster is made tangible by the image of wax which represents the power addressed, that is otherwise invisible. The ideal becomes concrete in the figure that is thus magically employed. It is in this magical sense that the opening chapters of the Ritual are declared to contain the "words of power" that bring about the resurrection and the glory of the Manes in Amenta. This mode of magic is likewise a mode of hypnotism or human magnetism which was universally common with the primitive races, especially the African, but which is only now being timidly touched by modern science. The power of paralyzing and of arresting motion was looked upon as magical potency indeed. Hypnotic power is magical power. This is described as being taken from the serpent as its strength. In one passage (Rit., ch. 149) the serpent is described as he "who paralyzes with his eyes". And previously, in the same chapter, the speaker says to the serpent, "I am the man who covers thy head with darkness, and I am the great magician. Thine eyes have been given to me, and I am glorified through them. Thy strength [or power] is in my grasp". This might be termed a lesson in hypnotism. The speaker becomes a great magician by taking possession of the paralyzing power in the eyes of the serpent. The description seems to imply that there had been a contest betwixt the serpent–charmer and the serpent, and that the man had conquered by wresting the magical power from the reptile. The Manes has much to say about the adversary of souls whom he meets in Amenta. This is the Apap of darkness, of drought and dearth, disease and death. It is the representative of evil in physical phenomena which was translated as a figure from the mythology into the domain of eschatology. In (chapter 32) the "Osiris standeth up upon his feet" to face and defy the crocodiles of darkness who devour the dead and carry off the words of power from the glorified in the under–world. They are stopped and turned back when the speaker says: "I am Atum. All things which exist are in my grasp, and those depend on me which are not yet in being. I have received increase of length and depth and fulness of breathing within the domain of my father the great one. He hath given me the beautiful Amenta through which the living pass from death to life" (ch.32). Thus the Osiris appears, speaks, and acts in the characters of a drama previously extant in the mythology. He comes forth: As the bull of Osiris (ch. 53A); as the god in lion form, Atum (ch. 54); as the jackal Ap–uat, of Sothis or Polaris; as the divine hawk, Horus (ch. 71); as the sacred hawk (ch. 78); as the lotus of earth (ch. 81); as the bennu–bird or phoenix–soul of Ra (ch. 83); as the shen–shen or hernshaw (ch. 84); as the soul that is an image of the eternal (ch. 85) as the dove or swallow (ch. 86); as the crocodile Sebek (ch. 88); as the khu, or glorified spirit (ch. 91); and many more. But the individual is shown to persist in a human form. He comes forth by day and is living after death in the figure, but not as the mummy, that he wore on earth. He is portrayed staff in hand, prepared for his journey through the under–world (Naville, *Todt.*, Kap 2, vignette). Also the ka–image of man the immortal is portrayed in the likeness of man the mortal. The human figure is never lost to view through all the phantasmagoria of transformation

(Naville, *Todt.*, vignettes to Kap 2 and 186). From beginning to end of the Ritual we see it is a being once human, man Or woman, who is the traveller through the nether–world up the mount of rebirth in heaven, at the summit of the stellar paradise, where the effigy of the earthly personality was ultimately merged in the divine image of the ka, and the mortal puts on immortality in the likeness of the dear old humanity, changed and glorified. This shows the ghost was founded on a human basis, and that it continued the human likeness in proof of its human origin.

Resurrection in the Ritual is the coming forth to day (Peri–em–hru), whether FROM the life on earth or to the life attainable in the heaven of eternity. The first resurrection is, as it were, an ascension from the tomb in the nether earth by means of the secret doorway. But this coming forth is *in*, not *from*, Amenta, after burial in the upper earth. The deceased had passed through the sepulchre, emerging in the lower earth. He issues from the valley of darkness and the shadow of death. Osiris had been cut to pieces in the lunar and other phenomena by the evil Sut, and the limbs were gathered up and put together by his son and by the mother in Amenta, where he rose again as Horus from the dead. And whatsoever had been postulated of

Osiris the mummy in the mythology was repeated on behalf of the Osiris in the eschatology.

Osiris had originated as a god in matter when the powers were elemental, but in the later theology the supreme soul in nature was configurated in a human form. Matter as human was then considered higher than matter unhumanized, and the body as human mummy was superior to matter in external nature. Also the spirit in human form was something beyond an elemental spirit; hence the god as supreme spirit was based, as already shown, upon the human ghost, with matter as the mummy. Osiris as a mummy in Amenta is what we might call the dead body of matter invested with the limbs and features of the human form, as the type to which the elemental powers had attained in Ptah, in Atum, and in the human featured Horus, which succeeded the earlier representation by means of zootypes. Osiris is a figure of inanimate nature, personalized as the mummy with a human form and face, whilst being also an image of matter as the physical body of the god. The process applied to the human body first in death was afterwards applied to the god in matter, in the elements, or in the inert condition at the time of the winter solstice, awaiting corpse–like for his transformation or transubstantiation into the young and glorious body of the sun, or spirit of vegetation in the spring. The solar god as the sun of evening or of autumn was the suffering, dying sun, or the dead sun buried in the nether earth. To show this, it was made a mummy of, bound up in the linen vesture without a seam, and thus imaged in a likeness of the dead who bore the mummy form on earth, the unknown being represented by the known. The sun god when descending to Amenta may be said to mummify or *karas* his own body in becoming earthed or, as it were, fleshed in the earth of Ptah. Hence the mummy–type of Ptah, of Atum, and Osiris, each of whom at different stages was the solar god in mummied form when buried in Amenta. It has now to be shown how it was brought about that the final and supreme one god of the Egyptian religion was represented as a mummy in the earth of eternity, and why the mystery of the mummy is the profoundest of all the mysteries of Amenta. An essential element in Egyptian religion was human sympathy with the suffering god, or the power in nature which gave itself, whether as herself or himself, as a living sacrifice, to bring the elements of life to men in light, in water, air, vegetation, fruit, roots, grain, and all things edible. Whence the type was eaten sacramentally at the *thanksgiving meal.* This feeling was pathetically expressed at "the festival of the staves", when crutches were offered as supports for the suffering autumn sun, otherwise the cripple deity Horus, dying down into Amenta and pitifully needing help which the human sympathizers tried to give. Can anything be more pathetic than this address to the sufferer as the sun god in Amenta: "Decree this, O Atum, that if I see thy face [in glory] I shall not be pained by the signs of thy sufferings". Atum decrees. He also decrees that the god will look on the suppliant as his second self (Rit., ch. 173; Naville).

The legend of the voluntary victim who in a passion of divinest pity became incarnate, and was clothed in human form and feature for the salvation of the world, did not originate in a belief that God had manifested once for all as an historic personage.It has its roots in the remotest part. The same legend was repeated in many lands with a change of name, and at times of sex, for the sufferer, but none of the initiated in the esoteric wisdom ever looked upon the Kamite Iusa, or gnostic Horus, Jesus, Tammuz, Krishna, Buddha, Witoba, or any other of the many saviours as historic in personality, for the simple reason that they had been more truly taught. Mythology was earlier than eschatology, and the human victim was preceded by the zootype; the phenomena first rendered mythically were not manifested in the human sphere. The natural genesis was in another category altogether. The earliest Horus was not incorporated in a human form. He represented that soul of life which came by water to a dried–up, withering world upon the verge of perishing with hunger and with thirst. Here the fish or the first–fruit of the earth was the sign of his incorporation in matter; hence the typical shoot, the green ear, or the branch that were imaged in Child–Horus. The saviour who came by water was Ichthys the fish. The saviour who came in fruit as product of the tree was the Natzer. The saviour who came by spirit was the soul of the sun. This was the earliest rendering of the incorporation of Horus as the primary life and light of the world made manifest in external nature, before the doctrine was applied to biology in the human domain, where Horus came by blood, as the mode of incarnation in the human form. In the later myth Osiris is the deity who suffered as the winter sun, assailed by all the powers of darkness. He also suffered from the drought as imaged in the fire–breathing Apap–reptile, and in other ways as lord of life in water, vegetation, and in various forms of food. This suffering deity or provider was the god in matter. Ra is the god in spirit, Osiris in matter. Not only in the matter of earth, but also in the human form – the form assumed by Horus as the child of earth, or Seb.

Osiris, the great sufferer in the dead of winter, was not simply the sun, nor was Osiris dead, however inert in matter, lying dumb in darkness, with non–beating heart. He was the buried life of earth, and hence the god in matter imaged in the likeness of a mummy waiting for the resurrection in Amenta. Such was the physical basis in the mythos of the mystery that is spiritual in the eschatology. Mummy–making in Egypt was far older than the Osirian cult. It was at least as old as Anup the divine embalmer of the dead. Preserving the human mummy perfectly intact was a mode of holding on to the individual form and features as a means of preserving the earthly likeness for identifying the personality hereafter in spirit. The mummy was made on purpose to preserve the physical likeness of the mortal. The risen dead are spoken of in the Ritual as "those who have found their faces". The mummy Was a primitive form of the African effigy in which the body was preserved as its own portrait, whereas the ka Was intended for a likeness of the spirit or immortal – the likeness in which the just spirit made perfect was to see Osiris in his glory. Both the mummy and the ka were represented in the Egyptian tomb, each with a chamber to itself. From the beginning there had been a visible endeavour to preserve some likeness or memento of the earthly body even when the bones alone could be preserved. Mummy–making in the Ritual begins with collecting the bones and piecing them together, if only in a likeness of the skeleton. It is at this stage that Horus is said to collect the bones of his father Osiris for the resurrection in a future life by means of transubstantiation. The same primitive mode of preparing the mummy is implied when it is said to the solar god on entering the under–world, "Reckon thou thy bones, and set thy limbs, and turn thy face to the beautiful Amenta" (ch. 133, Renouf). Teta, deceased, is thus addressed, "O Teta, thou hast raised up thy head for thy bones, and thou hast raised up thy bones for thy head". Also the hand of Teta is said to be like a wall as support of Horus in giving stability to his bones. Thus the foundation was laid for building the mummy–type as a present image of the person who had passed.

Amongst other types, the Yucatanese made little statues of their fathers. The head was left hollow, so that the ashes of the cremated body might be placed in the skull, as in an urn; this, says Landa, was then covered "with the skin of the occiput taken from the corpse". The custom is akin to that which has been unearthed in the European bone caves, where the skulls of the adult dead are found to have been trepanned, and the bones of little children inserted instead of human ashes. In Sign-language the bones of the child were typical of rebirth in a future life. The desire to live and the longing for a life after death, in earlier times, are inexpressible and the efforts made to give some kind of expression to the feeling are ineffably pathetic. D' Acugna relates that it was a custom with the South American Indians to preserve and keep the dead bodies of relatives in their homes as long as was possible, so as to have their friends continually before their eyes. For these they made feasts and set out viands before the dead bodies. Here, in passing, we would suggest that in the Egyptian custom as described by both Herodotus and Plutarch it was not the dead mummy that was brought to table as a type of immortality, but the image of the ka, which denoted what the guests would be like after death, and was therefore a cause for rejoicing. Carrying the ka image round the festive board was just a Kamite prototype of the elevation and carrying round of the host for adoration in the Church of Rome. Indeed, the total paraphernalia of the Christian mysteries had been made use of in Egyptian temples. For instance, in one of the many titles of Osiris in all his forms and places he is called *"Osiris in the monstrance"* (Rit., ch. 141, Naville). In the Roman ritual the monstrance is a transparent vessel in which the host or victim is exhibited. In the Egyptian cult Osiris was the victim. The elevation of the host signifies the resurrection of the crucified god, who rose again in spirit from the *corpus* of the victim, now represented by the host. Osiris in the monstrance should of itself suffice to show that the Egyptian Karast (Krst) is the original Christ, and that the Egyptian mysteries were continued by the gnostics and Christianized in Rome. The mode of conveying the oral wisdom to the initiate in the mysteries of young man making was continued in the mystery of mummy making. Whilst the mummy was being prepared for burial, chapters of the Ritual were read to it, or to the conscious ka, by an official who was known as the man of the roll. Every Egyptian was supposed to be acquainted with the formula, from having learned them during his lifetime, by which he was to have the use of his limbs and possession of his soul restored to him in death, and to be protected from the dangers of the nether–world. These were repeated to the dead person, however, for greater security, during the process of embalming, and the son of the deceased, or the master of the ceremonies, took care to whisper to the mummy the most mysterious parts, which no living ear might hear with impunity. (Maspero, *The Struggle of the Nations*, Eng. trans., pp. 510, 5 I I.)

But it is an error to suppose with some Egyptologists, like M. de Horrack, that the new existence of the deceased was begun in the old earthly body (*Proceed. Society of Bib. Archaeology*, vol. vi., March 4, 1884, p. 126). The resurrection of the dead in mummy form may look at first sight as if the old dead corpse had risen from the sepulchre. But the risen is not the dead mummy, it is a type of personality in the shape of the mummy. It is what the Ritual describes as the mummy–form of a god. The Manes prays, "May I too arise and assume the mummied form as a god", that is, as the mummy of Osiris, the form in which Amsu–Horus rose, a type of permanent preservation, but not yet one of the spirits made perfect by possession of the ka. It was this mistake which led to a false idea that the Egyptians held the dogma of a corporeal resurrection of the dead which became one of the doctrines that were fostered into fixity by the A–Gnostic Christians. The Osiris as mortal Manes, or Amsu–Horus as divinity, does rise in the mummy form, but this is in another life and in another world, not as a human being on our earth. It has the look of a physical resurrection in the old body, and so the ignorant misinterpreters mistook it and founded on it a corporeal basis for the future life. In the Christian scheme the buried dead were to rise again in the old physical *corpus* for the last judgment in time at the literal ending of the world. This was another delusion based on the misrendering of the Egyptian wisdom. The dead who rose again in Amenta, which was the ground floor of a future state of existence, also rose again for the judgment; but this took place in the earth of eternity which was mistaken by the Christians for the earth of time, just as they had mistaken the form of the risen sahu for the old body of matter that never was supposed to rise again by those who knew. The earthly mummy of the deceased does not go to heaven, nor does it enter the solar boat, yet the Osiris is told to enter the boat, his reward being the *seat which receives his sahu or spirit mummy* (Rit., ch. 130). Clearly this can only refer to the spiritual body, as the earthly mummy was left on the earth outside the gates of Amenta. Not only is the corporeal mummy not placed on board the boat of souls, the deceased was to be represented by a statue of cedar wood anointed with oil, or, as we might say, *Christified* (134,9, 10).There is no possible question of a corporeal resurrection. The object, aim, and end of all the spiritualizing processes is to become non-corporeal in the earthly sense — that is, as the Ritual represents it, to defecate into pure spirit. The word sahu (or the mummy) is employed to express the future form as well as the old. But it is a spiritual sahu, the divine mummy. Even the bones and flesh of souls are mentioned but these are the bones of Osiris, the backbone of the universal frame, and the flesh of Ra. The terms used for the purpose of divinizing are antipodal to any idea of return to corporeality as a material mummy. The mummy of the Manes is a sahu of the glorified spirit. This state of being is attained by the deceased in chapter 73: "I am the *beloved son* of his father. I come to the state of a sahu of the well-furnished Manes". He is said to be mummified in the shape of a divine hawk when he takes the form of Horus (78, 15, 16), not as the earthly mummy in a resurrection on our earth. The resurrection of Osiris was not corporeal. The mummy of the god in matter or mortality rises from the tomb transubstantiated into spirit. So complete is the transformation that he is Osiris bodily changed into Horus as a sahu or spirit. The Egyptians had no doctrine of a physical resurrection of the dead. Though they retained the mummy *as a type of personality*, it was a changed and glorified *form* of the earthly body, the mummy that had attained its feet in the resurrection. It was the Karast mummy, or, word for word and thing for thing,

Amsu–Horus was the Kamite Christ who rose up from the mummy as a spirit.

Also it is entirely false to represent the Egyptians as making the mummy and preserving it for the return of the soul into the old earthly body. That is but a shadow of the true idea cast backwards by Christianity. Millions of cats were made into mummies and sacredly preserved around the city of Bubastes, but not with the notion of a bodily resurrection. They were the totems of the great cat clan or its metropolis, the Egyptian "Clan Chattan", which had become symbols or fetishes of religious significance to later times when the totemic mother as the cat, the seer by night, was divinized in the lunar goddess Pasht, and the worshippers embalmed her zootype, not because they adored the cat, but because the deess herself was the Great Mother typified by the cat. Both the mother and the moon were recognized beyond the cat, which was their totemic zootype and venerated symbol. Osiris was the mummy of Amenta in two characters; in one he is the khat–mummy lying laid out with corpse–like face upon the funeral couch, in the other he is the mummy risen to his feet and reincorporated in the glorious body. These two characters were continued as the *Corpus Christi* and the risen Christ in Rome. Hence in the iconography of the catacombs the

Egyptian mummy as Osiris–sahu, and as Horus the new–born solar child, are the demonstrators of the resurrection for the Christian faith, where there is no testimony whatever to an historical event. Any time during the last 10,000 years the mummy made for burial in the tomb was imaged in the likeness of Osiris in Amenta, who, though periodically buried, rose again for ever as the type of life eternal. In making the mummy of Osiris the Egyptians were also making an image of the god who rose again in spirit as Osiris–sahu or as Horus divinized, the risen Christ of the Osirian cult. When the lustrations were performed with water in Tattu and the anointings with oil in Abydos, it was what may be termed a mode of Christifying or making Horus the child of earth into Horus the son of god who became so in his baptism and anointing that were represented in the mysteries. The first Horus was born of the virgin, not begotten. The second Horus was begotten of the father, and the child was made a man of in his baptismal regeneration with the water and with unction, with the oil of a tree or the fat of a bull.

We have now to show that in making the mummy the Egyptians were also making the typical Christ, which is the anointed. The word karas, kares, or karis in Egyptian signifies embalmment, to embalm, to anoint, *to make the mummy. Kreas, creas, or chros,* in Greek denotes the human body, a person or carcase, more expressly the flesh of it; *cras,* Gaelic and Irish, the body; Latin, *corpus,* for a dead body; these are all preceded by the word karas or karast, in Egyptian, with the risen mummy for determinative of the meaning. Each body that had been embalmed was karast, so to say, and made into a type of immortality in the likeness of Osiris–sahu or Horus, the prototypal Christ. It will be made apparent by degrees that the religion of the Chrestoi first began at Memphis with the cultus of the mummy in its two characters, which represented body and spirit, or Ptah in matter and Kheper(Iu–em–hetep) in spirit. Hence the hawk as bird of spirit issuing from the karast–mummy was an image of the resurrection. The origin of the Christ as the anointed or "karast" will explain the connection of the Christ name and that of the Christiani with unction and anointing. Horus the Kamite Christ was the anointed son. The oil upon his face was the sign of his divinity. This supplied a figure of the Christ to Paul when he says that for those who *"put on Christ"* "there can be no male and female, for ye are one [man or mummy] in Christ Jesus" (Gal., iii. 28). The Christ was "put on" metaphorically in the process of anointing which originated with the making of the mummy. Whether the dead were represented by the bones invested with a coating of blood, of flesh-coloured earth, or by the eviscerated and desiccated body that was bandaged in the cloth of a thousand folds, the object was to preserve and perpetuate the deceased in some permanent form of personality. The Egyptians aimed at making the mummy imperishable and incorruptible, as an image of durability and continuity, a type of the eternal, or of Osiris–karast in the likeness of a mummy. Hence the swathe without a seam and of incredible length in which the mummy was enfolded to represent unending duration. Some of these have been unwound to the extent of seven or eight hundred yards, and one of them is described as being a thousand yards in length. But, however long, it was made without a seam. This vesture is alluded to in the chapter of the golden vulture. The chapter is to be inscribed for the protection of the deceased on "the day of his burial in the cloth of a thousand folds" (Rit., ch. 157 1 3).

This cloth was the seamless swathe of the Egyptian *karast*, which became the vesture or "coat without a seam woven from the top throughout "(John, xix. 23) for the Christ. Even the poorest Egyptian, whose body was steeped in salt and natron and anointed with a little cedar oil, was wrapped in a single piece of linen equally with the mummy whose swathe was hundreds of yards in length, because the funeral vesture of Osiris, his body of matter, was without a seam. The dead are often called "the bandaged ones". On rising from the tomb the deceased exclaims triumphantly, "O my father! my sister! my mother Isis! I am freed from my bandages ! I can see ! I am one of those who are freed from their bandages to see Seb" (158, I). Seb denotes the earth, and the Manes is free to visit the earth again, this time as the ghost or double of his former self. Covering the corpse with the transparent tahn, or golden gum, was one way of turning the dead body into a type of the spiritual body which was imaged as the glorified. One cannot doubt that this was a mode of showing the transformation of the Osirian dead mummy into the luminous body called the sahu of Osiris when he was transfigured but still retained the mummy form in Amsu–Horus at his rising from the sepulchre. Mummies buried in the tomb at Medum had been thus enveloped. This was one form of investiture alluded to in the Ritual as distinguished from the mummy bandages. One of these mummies is now to be seen in the Royal College of Surgeons. "The mode of embalming", says Prof. Petrie, "was very singular. The body was shrunk, wrapped up in linen cloth, then modelled all over with resin (or tahn) into the natural shape and plumpness of the living figure, completely restoring all the fullness of the form, and this was wrapped round with a few turns of the finest gauze". (Petrie, *Medum*, Introduction, chapter 2, pages 17 and 18.) There was no coffin present in the tomb. The mummy thus invested with the tahn had been buried in this primitive kind of glass case, in which the form and features could be seen either directly or by means of the modelling. The tahn, gum or resin, as a natural product from the tree, preceded glass, and would be fashioned for the earlier monstrance. Remodelling the dead in the likeness of the living form by means of the pellucid tahn is a mode of making the glorified body on earth that was imaged by the sahu in Amenta, and thus the mummy here attains the two–fold type of the Osiris Khat, or corpse, and the Osiris–sahu, or the glorified in spirit. In the Christian agglomerate of Egyptian doctrines and dogmas, rites and symbols, the pellucid tahn may, we think, be recognized in the sacred monstrance of the Roman ritual. This is a show–case in which the host or *Corpus Christi* is placed to be uplifted and exhibited. The eye of Horus is yet visible in the *lanula* or crescent–shaped crystal of the monstrance which holds the consecrated bread. The name of this show–case is derived from the Latin *monstrare*, "to show", and this had been the object of the mummy makers in employing the transparent tahn.

In the eschatological or final phase of the doctrine, to make the mummy was to make the typical anointed, also called the Messu, the Messiah, and the Christ. Mes or mas, in the hieroglyphics, signifies to anoint and to steep, as in making the mummy, and messu in Egyptian means the anointed; whence lah the Messu becomes Messiah in Hebrew. There was a previous form of the anointed in the totemic mysteries of young man making. When the boy attained the age of puberty he was made into the anointed one at the time of his initiation into the way of a man with a woman. It was a custom with certain Inner African tribes to slit the urethra of the boy and lubricate the member with palm oil. This was a primitive way of making the anointed at puberty. Australian aborigines are also known to slit the prepuce cover for the same purpose. At this stage of the mystery the anointed one is the adult youth who has attained the rank of begetter full of grace and favour, or is khemt, as it was rendered in Egyptian. Tertullian claims that the name of the Christians came from the unction received by Jesus Christ. This is in perfect keeping with the derivation of the typical Christ from the mummy which was anointed so abundantly with oil in its embalmment. It is said of the woman who anointed Jesus in Bethany," in that she poured the ointment upon my body, she did it *to prepare me for my burial* " (Matt. xxvi. 12). She was preparing the mummy after the manner of Anup the embalmer, who prepared Osiris for his burial and resurrection. But it was only as a dead mummy and not a living man that the gnostic Jesus could have been embalmed for burial.

We now proceed to show that Christ the anointed is none. other than the Osiris–karast, and that the karast mummy risen to its feet as Osiris–sahu was the prototypal Christ. Unhappily , these demonstrations cannot be made without a wearisome mass of detail. And we are bound for the bottom this time. Dr. Budge, in his book on the mummy, tells his readers that the Egyptian word for mummy is *ges*, which signifies to wrap up in bandages. But he does not point out that ges or kes, to embalm the corpse or make the mummy, is a reduced or abraded form of an earlier word, karas (whence krst for the mummy). The original word written in hieroglyphics is ,.krst, whence kas, to embalm, to bandage, to knot, to make the mummy or karast (Birch, *Dictionary of the Hieroglyphics*, pp. 415–416; Champollion, *Gram. Egyptienne*, 86).

The Mummy-Babe.

The word krs denotes the embalmment of the mummy, and the krst, as the mummy, was made in the process of preparation by purifying, anointing, and embalming. To karas the dead body was to embalm it, to bandage it, to make the mummy. The mummy was the Osirian *Corpus Christi*, prepared for burial as the laid–out dead, the karast by name. When raised to its feet, it was the risen mummy, or sahu. The place of embalmment was likewise the krs. Thus the process of making the mummy was to karas, the place in which it was laid is the karas, and the product was the krst, whose image is the upright mummy = the risen Christ. Hence the name of the Christ, Christos in Greek, Chrestus in Latin, for the anointed, was derived, as the present writer previously suggested, from the Egyptian word krst. Karas also signifies the burial–place, and the word modifies into Kâs or Châs. Kâsu the burial place "was a name of the 14th Nome in Upper Egypt. A god Kâs is mentioned three or four times in the Book of the Dead, the god Kâs who is in the Tuat" (ch. 40). This was a title of the mummy Osiris in the funerary dwelling. In one passage Kâs is described as the deliverer or saviour from all mortal needs. In "the chapter of raising the body" (178) it is said of the deceased that he had been hungry and thirsty (on earth), but he will (never hunger or thirst any more, "for Kâs delivers him" and does away with wants like these. That is, in the resurrection. Here the name of the god Osiris–Kâs written at full is Osiris the Karast – the Egyptian Christ. Not only is the risen mummy or sahu called the karast, Osiris as lord of the bier is the Neb–karast equivalent to the later Christ the Lord, and the lord of the bier is god of the resurrection from the house of death. The karast is literally the god or person who has been mummified, embalmed, and anointed or christified. Anup the baptizer and embalmer of the dead for the new life was the preparer of the karast–mummy. As John the Baptist is the founder of the Christ in baptism, so Anup was the *christifier* of the mortal Horus, he on whom the holy ghost descended as a bird when the Osiris made his transformation in the marriage mystery of Tat tu (Rit., ch. 17). We read in the funeral texts of Anup– being "Suten tu hetep, Anup, neb tser khent neter ta *krast*–ef em set" (Birch, *Funereal Text* 4th Dynasty). "Suten hept tu Anup tep–tuf khent neter ha am ut neb tser *krast* ef em as–ef en kar neter em set Amenta" (Birch, *Funereal Stele of Ra–Khepr–Ka*, 12th Dynasty). Anup gives embalmment, krast; he is lord over the place of embalmment, the kras ; the lord of embalming (krast), who, so to say, makes the "krast". The process of embalmment is to make the mummy. This was a type of immortality or rising again.Osiris is krast, or embalmed and mummified for the resurrection. Passage into life and light is made for the karast–dead through the embalmment of the good Osiris (Rit., ch. 162)–that is, through his being karast as the mummy type. Thus the Egyptian krast was the pre–Christian Christ, and the pictures in the Roman Catacombs preserve the proof. The passing of the karast into the Christ is depicted in the gnostic iconography. It is in the form of a child bound up in the swathings of a diminutive Egyptian mummy, with the halo and cross of the four quarters round its head, which show its solar origin. It is the divine infant which has the head of Ra in the Ritual who says, "I am the babe; I renew myself, and I grow young again" (chs. 42 and 43). The karast mummy is the type of resurrection in the Roman Catacombs because the karast was the prototypal Christ. It is the Egyptian karast as thing and word that supplied and will explain the Greek Christ, Christos, Krstos, or Latin Chrestus and account for the *Corpus Christi*, the anointed, the Saviour, doctrinally, typically, actually in every way except historically, and of that the karast, Krstos, or Christ is entirely independent. "Henceforth", said a dignitary of the Church of England the other day, "Christianity has done with the metaphysical Christ". But there is no physical Christ except the karast mummy, which was Osiris when laid out and lying down in death, and Horus of the resurrection standing up as Amsu risen from the sepulchre, having the whip hand over all the powers of darkness and the adversaries of his father.

Say what you will or believe what you may, there is no other origin for Christ the anointed than for Horus the karast or anointed son of god the father. There is no other origin for a Messiah as the anointed than for the Masu or anointed. Finally, then, the mystery of the mummy is the mystery of the Christ. As Christian, it is allowed to be for ever inexplicable. As Osirian, the mystery can be explained. It is one of the mysteries of Amenta, with a more primitive origin in the rites of totemism.

We now claim sufficient warrant for affirming that Christ the anointed is a mystical figure which originated as the Egyptian mummy in the twofold character of Osiris in his death and in his resurrection;

as Osiris, or mortal Horus, the karast; and Osiris–sahu, or Horus divinized as the anointed son. The Christ or karast still continues to be made when the sacrament of extreme unction is administered to the dying as a Roman Catholic rite. Though but a shadow of the primitive reality, it perpetuates the "sacred mystery" of converting the corpse into the sahu, the transubstantiation of the inert Osiris by descent of Ra; the mortal Horus, child of the mother, into Horus the anointed son of god the father. "Extreme unction", the seventh of the holy sacraments, is indeed a Christian rite.

It will now be necessary to give an account of certain other mysteries of Amenta and doctrines of the Ritual. The Egyptians celebrated ten great mysteries on ten different nights of the year. The first was the night of the evening meal (literally the last supper), and the laying of offerings on the altar. It is the night of provisioning the Lord's table. Osiris had been overcome by Sut and the Sebau, who had once more renewed their assault upon Un–nefer when they were defeated and exterminated by his faithful followers. Therefore this was also the night of the great battle when the moon god Taht and the children of light annihilated the rebellious powers of darkness. On the second night the overthrown Tat–Cross, with Osiris in it, or on it, was again erected by Horus, Prince of Sekhem, in the region of Tat tu, where the holy spirit Ra descends upon the mummy and the twain become united for the resurrection. On the third night the scene is in "Sekhem; the mystery is that of the blind Horus or of Horus in the dark, who here receives his sight. It is also the mystery of dawn upon the coffin of Osiris. We might call it the mystery of Horus the mortal transfiguring into Horus the immortal. On the fourth night the four pillars are erected with which the future kingdom of god the father is to be founded. It is called "the night of erecting the flag–staffs of Horus, and of establishing him as the heir of his father's property". The fifth scene is in the region of Rekhet, and the mystery is that of the two sisters with Isis watching in tears over her brother Osiris, and brooding above the dead body to give it the warmth of new life. On the sixth night the glorious ones are judged, the evil dead are parted off, and joy goeth its round in Thinnis. This is the night of the great festival named *Ha–k–er–a*, or "Come thou to me", in which the blending of the two souls was solemnized as a glorious mystery by a festival at which there was much eating and drinking. The mystery of the seventh night was that of the great judgment on the highway of the damned, when the suit was closed against the rebels who had failed once more and were ignominiously defeated. After the verdict comes the avengement. The eighth is the night of the great hoeing in Tat tu, when the associates of Sut are massacred and the fields are manured with their blood. The ninth is called "the night of hiding the body of him who is supreme in attributes". The mystery is that of collecting the remains of Osiris, whose body was mutilated and scattered piecemeal by Sut, and of *hiding* it. The mystery on the tenth night presents a picture of Anup, the embalmer, the anointer, or christifier of the mummy. This is in Rusta, the place of resurrection from Amenta. It may be the series is not in exact order, but that does not interfere with the nature of the mysteries. In each of the ten acts of the drama the suffering Osiris and the triumph over all his adversaries are portrayed as mysteries in a prototypal miracle–play or drama that was held to be divine. The chapter of these ten mysteries was recited penitentially for the purification of the Manes and the coming forth after death (Rit., ch. 18, rubric). With this we may compare the fact that the Jewish new year is ushered in with ten days of penitence.

The altar or communion–table thus provisioned was the coffin lid. This also was continued in the ritual of Rome, for it is a fact that the earliest Christian altar was a coffin. According to Blunt's *Dictionary of Doctrinal and Historical Theology* (p. 16), this was a hollow chest, on the lid or *mensa* of which the eucharist was celebrated. This, as Egyptian, was the coffin of Osiris that constituted the altar on which the provisions were laid in Sekhem for the eucharistic meal. Hence the resurrection is described as "dawn upon the coffin of Osiris". Therefore he rose in spirit from the mummy in the coffin, beneath the lid which constituted the table. This was the body supposed to be eaten as the eucharist, which was represented by the provisions that were laid upon the altar for the sacramental meal. The first of the ten great mysteries is the mystery of the eucharist, and we find that the primitive Christian liturgies are all and wholly restricted to the eucharist as the one primordial sacrament of the Christian Church. The first of the Osirian mysteries is the primary Christian sacrament. "Provisioning the altar" was continued by the Church of Rome."The mysteries laid upon the altar "which preceded" the communion of the body and blood of Christ "were then eaten in the eucharistic meal". (Neale, Rev. J. M., *The Liturgies*, Introd., p. 33). Thus we see in the *camera obscura* that the provisions laid on the altar or table represented the flesh and blood of the victim about to be eaten sacramentally. The night of the things that were laid upon the altar is the night of the great sacrifice, with Osiris as the victim. The things laid on the altar for the evening meal represented the body and blood of the Lord. These, as the bread and wine, or flesh and beer, were trans-elemented or transub-stantiated by the descent of Ra the holy spirit, which quickened and transformed the mummy Osiris into the risen sahu, the unleavened bread into the leavened, the water into wine. Osiris, the sacrifice, was the giver of himself as "the food which never perishes". (Rit., ch. 89).

The Christian liturgies are reckoned to be the "most pure sources of eucharistical doctrine". And liturgy appears to have been the groundwork of the Egyptian ritual. It is said by one of the priests (Rit., ch. I), "I am he who reciteth the liturgies of the soul who is lord of Tattu" – that is, of Osiris who establishes a soul for ever in conjunction with Ra the holy spirit in the mysteries of Amenta. In one character Osiris was eaten as the Bull of Eternity, who gave his flesh and blood as sustenance for humanity, and who was the divine providence as the provider of food. The eating of the mother was also continued in the eucharist, Osiris being of both sexes. This was typically fulfilled in one way by converting the bull into an ox. The duality was also imaged in the bread and beer or wine, which is the mother blood in a commuted guise. It is said of the body that was eaten in "the Roman mysteries" that it is "the body which bestows on us, *out of its wounds*, immortality and life, and the beatific vision with the angels, and food and drink, and life and light, the very bread of life, the true light, eternal life, Christ. Jesus". "Wherefore this entrance symbolizes at the same time both the second advent of Christ and His sepulture, for it is He who will be our beatific vision in the life to come", as Horus of the second sight, all of which was portrayed of Osiris and fulfilled. (Neale, *The Liturgies, Introd.*, p. 30.) Blood sacrifice from the beginning was an offering of life, hence the life offering. When the mother was the victim her blood was offered as life to the ancestral spirits. It was also life to the brotherhood, and partaking of it in communion constituted the sacrament. So in the Christian eucharist the blood is taken to be the life, and is partaken of as the life, the "life of the world" (Neale, *Liturgy of Basil the Great*), "the divine life that is the life everlasting, the new life that is for ever" (Neale, *Liturgy of St. Chrysostom*, ii.). The bread broken in the Christian sacrament represents a body that was "*broken, immolated, and divided*". This does not apply to the body of Jesus, according to the "history". But it does apply to the body of Osiris, which was "broken, immolated, and divided" by Sut, who tore it into fourteen fragments. The altar table, or coffin lid, was provisioned with these parts of the broken body to be typically eaten as the eucharist on the night "when there are at the coffin the thigh, the head, the heel, and the leg of Un–nefer". Moreover, when the mother was eaten as the sacrifice, the flesh and blood were warm with life. She was not eaten in cold blood. It was the same with the Meriah of the Kolarians, and also with the totemic animal. The efficacy lay in the flesh being eaten alive, and the blood being drunk whilst it was warm with life which constituted the "living sacrifice". This type of sacrifice was also continued in the Christian eucharist. *Hot water was at one time poured into the chalice with the wine at the consecration of the elements, to give it the warmth of life* (Neale, *Liturgy of St. Chrysostom, p. 120.*) Even the act of tearing the flesh of the victim's body piecemeal is piously perpetuated by the breaking instead of cutting the bread for the Christian sacrament. The lights upon the coffin of Osiris are represented in the Roman ritual by a double taper, the *dikerion*, reputed to signify *"the advent of the Holy Spirit"*, which corresponds to the descent of Ra the holy spirit on the inert body of Osiris in Tattu, where the two souls are blended to become one in Horus of the resurrection.

The flabellum or fan is a mystical emblem in the Egyptian mysteries. For one thing, it signified the shade or spirit. Fans are frequently portrayed for souls of a primitive type. (Birch, *Trans. Soc. Bib. Arch.*, vol. viii., p. 386.) Souls burning in the hells are imaged by flabella. These fans were brought on in the Oriental Church. In the Clementine liturgy they are ordered to be made of peacocks' feathers (Neale, p. 76, Introd., pp. 29, 30). They are called fans of the Holy Spirit, and were carried in procession with the "veil that was wrapped about the body of the Lord Jesus" like the folds of gauze that were wrapped round the mummy at Medum. But the fan or shade = spirit had been reduced in status, and was then used as a flapper for whisking the flies away from the sacrifice (Durandus, iv, 33–8; Neale, Introduction, page 29). It is not pretended that the second advent is historical, nevertheless it is portrayed in the mystery of the eucharist by the descent of the Holy Spirit. The second advent is the coming forth of Horus in spirit from the mummy or corpse which was his image in the human form. The first is in being made flesh and putting on the likeness of mortality, the second is in making his transformation into a spirit, as the type of immortality. The marriage of Cupid and Psyche is a fable that was founded on this union of the two souls which we have traced in the Ritual as the soul in matter, or the human soul, and the soul in spirit. Cupid, under another name, is Eros, whilst Eros and Anteros are a form of the double Horus, Eros in spirit, Anteros in matter, and the blending of the two in the mysteries was the marriage of Cupid and Psyche in the mystery of Tattu. Now here is another of those many mysteries which have no origin in historic Christianity. The agape was celebrated in connection with the eucharist. This was not founded at the time of the Last Supper, nevertheless it was held to be a Christian sacrament. Paul in speaking of the love–feast at Corinth as a scene of drunken revelry (1. Cor. ii. 20–22), recognizes the celebration of two suppers, which he is desirous of having kept apart, one for the church, and one for the house. These two are the eucharist and the agape. Ecclesiastical writers differ as to which of the two ought to be solemnized first, but there is no question that two were celebrated in connection with each other. In his attack on the licentiousness of the Christian agape Tertullian asks the wives, "Will not your husbands know what it is you secretly take before other food?" and again, "Who will without anxiety endure her absence all night long at the Pascal solemnities?". "Who will without some suspicion of his own let her go to attend that Lord's banquet which they defame?" (Keating, Y. F., *The Agape and the Eucharist*, p. 70.) As Egyptian, we can identify the two, and thus infer the order in which they stood to each other. Whether both were called suppers or not, the Egyptians celebrated the last supper of Osiris on the last night of the old year, and the mesiu, or the evening meal, on the first night of the new year. And this duality was maintained by the gnostics and continued by the Christians. These are two of the Osirian mysteries, and in the list of the ten great mysteries there are two nights of provisioning the altar – that is, two nights of a feast or memorial supper. One is held in Annu, the other in Sekhem, with the resurrection in Tattu coming between the two. In Sekhem the blind Horus receives his sight, or his beatific vision of the divine glory, which was seen when he had pierced the veil hawk–headed in the image of Ra. Provisioning the altar in Sekhem is designated "dawn upon the coffin of Osiris" (Rit., ch. 18). The eucharist was a form of the mortuary meal in which the death of Osiris was commemorated by the eating of the body and the drinking of the blood. The agape, or phallic feast, was a mode of celebrating the re–arising of Horus, Prince of Sekhem, as portrayed by the re-erection of the Tat. This accounts for the sexual orgie of the agape, a primitive form of which was acted by the Eskimo in the festival of reproduction. In their mysteries this was the reproduction of food. In the Egyptian it was the regeneration and resurrection of the soul that was celebrated at the agape. The death, of course, came first. This was on the night of the great sacrifice, and the eucharist was eaten in commemoration. Then followed the triumph in Tattu and the regenesis of the soul, which was acted by the "holy kiss" or blending of the sexes in the feast of love, as a dramatic rendering of this union betwixt the human nature and divine, or of the brother and sister, Shu and Tefnut. In the totemic mysteries of young man making begettal was included in the *modus operandi,* and in this the women invoked the spirit of the male for the new birth. The phallic festival of promiscuous intercourse still survived when the mysteries became religious, whether in Egypt, Greece, or Rome. In these Osiris was resuscitated as Horus the only begotten son, the women being the begetters or regenerators. In the evocations of Isis and Nephthys we hear them calling on the lost Osiris to come back to them in the person of the son. They plead that the lamp of life may be relighted, or more literally that the womb may be replenished". Come to thine abode, god An", they cry. "Beloved of the Adytum! Come to Kha" (a name of phallic significance), "oh, fructifying Bull". This is in the beneficent formulae that were made by the two divine sisters, Isis and Nephthys, to effect the resurrection of Osiris, which are said to have been composed by them on the twenty–fifth day of the month Koiak, December 22nd. They are magical evocations of the god addressed to the inert Osiris, who is caused to rise again by Isis in his ithyphallic form. Most pathetic in its primitiveness is the picture of the two divine sisters, or mothers, Isis and Nephthys, watching by the dead or inert brother who is Osiris in death and Horus in his resurrection, crooning their incantations, brooding bird–like over the germ of life in the egg, and breathing out the very soul of their own life in yearning for him, until the first token of returning consciousness is given, the earliest sign of the resurrection is made in response to the vitalizing warmth of their affection. These evocations follow the night of "the last supper" and the battle with Sut and the Sebau. "Oh, come to thine abode!" the two dear sisters cry. "Come to thy sister! Come to thy wife! Come to thy spouse!" they plead whilst stretching out their longing arms for his embrace. "Oh, excellent Sovereign, come to thine abode. Rejoice; all thine enemies are annihilated. Thy two sisters are near to thee, protecting thy funeral couch, calling thee in weeping, thou who art prostrate on thy funeral bed. Thou seest our tender solicitude. Speak to us, Supreme Ruler, our Lord. Chase away all the anguish which is in our hearts". These in the funeral scenes are the two women watching in the tomb (*Records*, vol. ii.,119). Then was the only son of god begotten of the holy spirit Ra. The "pair of souls" were blended in the Horus of a soul that was to live for ever, or to taste eternal life. The marriage rite was acted, and the marriage feast was celebrated in this prototypal ceremony that was continued in the Agape of the Osirian and the Christian cult.

The Christian dogma of a physical resurrection founded on the historic fact of a dead corpse rising from the grave can be explained as one of the Kamite mysteries which were reproduced as miracles in the Gospels. If we take the original representation in the solar mythos, the sun in the under–world, the diminished, unvirile, impotent or suffering sun was imaged as Ans–Ra, the solar god bound up in linen, as the mummified Osiris. The type remained for permanent use, but when the transformation had been effected the mummy vanished. The sepulchre was empty. The sun of winter or of night did not remain in

Hades. Neither did it come forth as the dead body or unbreathing mummy of Osiris. Osiris, the hidden god in the earth of Amenta, does not come forth at all except in the person of the risen Horus, who is the manifestor for the ever–hidden father. To issue thus he makes his transfiguration which constitutes the mystery, not the miracle, of the resurrection. Osiris defecates and spiritualizes. The mummy as *corpus* is transubstantiated into the sahu, the mortal Horus into the immortal, and the physical mummy disappears. But it did not disappear because the living Horus rose up and walked off with the dead body of Osiris. When the transformation took place the type was changed in a moment, in the "twinkling of an eye". The mummy Osiris transubstantiates, and makes his transformation into Osiris–sahu. As the Ritual expresses it, "he is renewed in an instant" in this second birth (ch. 182). The place was empty where the mummy had lain upon the bier, and the body was not found. This change is described when it is said in the litany of Ra, he "raises his soul and hides his body". Thus the body was hidden in the resurrection of the soul. "Hiding his body" is consequently a name of Horus, "emanating from Hes" as a babe in the renewal of Osiris. Concealing the body of dead matter was one way of describing the transubstantiation in texture and the transfiguration in form. This was one of the greater mysteries.

When Horus rent the veil of the tabernacle he had become hawk–headed, and consequently was a spirit in the divine likeness of Ra the holy ghost. Therefore the tabernacle was the body or mummy, "the veil of flesh" (Neale, *Liturgy of St. James*, pp. 46–7) from which he had emerged. The speaker in the Ritual says, "I am the hawk in the tabernacle, and I pierce through the veil" – that is, when he is invested with the soul of Horus and disrobes himself of the mummy (Rit., ch. 71, Renouf) or the veil which represented the flesh, as did the veil of gauze when folded round the mummy in the pyramid at Medum. The "holy veil" was carried in the Christian mysteries, together with the "holy gifts" and "fans of the spirit", and this is said to represent "the veil that was wrapped about the body of the Lord Jesus" (Neale, *The Liturgies*, Introduction, page 30, "Prayer of the Veil".) This (in the *Liturgy of St. James*, Neale, page 46) is "the veil of the flesh of Christ", therefore the veil of the body or temple of the spirit that was rent in the resurrection by Horus when he "pierced through the veil". He rends or pierces through the veil, saying, "I am the hawk in the tabernacle, and I pierce through the veil. Here is Horus!" who comes forth to the day as a hawk (ch. 71

). In the form of a divine hawk the risen one is revealed and goes forth as a spirit. In the Gospel the loud cry is immediately followed by the going forth as a spirit. "And behold, the veil of the sanctuary was rent in twain from the top to the bottom. And the earth did quake, and the rocks were rent and the tombs were opened, and many bodies of the saints that had fallen asleep were raised (Matt. xxvii. 45–53). Horus now takes his seat at the table of his father Osiris, with those who eat bread in Annu. He gives breath to the faithful dead who are raised by him, he who is the resurrection and the life. The same scene is apparently reproduced by John. Jesus makes his apparition to the disciples at what looks like the evening meal, although the meal is not mentioned. Jesus is the breather. "He breathed on them and said, Receive ye the Holy Spirit" – which in the Ritual is the breath of Atum–Ra, the father, imparted by Iu the son, or by Horus to the faithful dead. The scene has now been changed from Amenta to the earth of Seb by those who made "historic" mockery of the Egyptian Ritual, and sank the meaning out of sight where it has been so long submerged. More of this hereafter. Enough at present to indicate the way that things are tending. In this divine drama natural realities are represented with no perniciously destructive attempt to conceal the characters under a mask of history. Majestically moving in their own might of pathetic appeal to human sympathy, they are simply represented for what they may be worth when rightly apprehended. But so tremendous was this tragedy in the Osirian mysteries, so heart–melting the legend of divinest pity that lived on with its rootage in Amenta and its flowerage in the human mind, that an historic travesty has kept the stage and held the tearful gaze of generation after generation for nineteen hundred years.

Amenta, the earth of eternity, is the land of the mysteries where Taht, the moon god, in the nether night was the great teacher of the sacred secrets together with the seven wise masters. The passage through Amenta is a series of initiations for the Osiris deceased. He is inducted into the mysteries of Rusta (I, 7, 9), the mysteries of the Tuat (130, 27), the mysteries of Akar (148, 2, 3). He knows the mysteries of Nekhen (I 13, I). Deceased invokes the god who dwells in all mysteries (14, I); deceased learns the mystery of the father god Atum, who becomes his own son (15,46); he is the mysterious of form (17, 91) and the mysterious of face, like Osiris (133,9). "I shine in the egg", says the deceased, "in the land of the mysteries". Chapter 162 contains the most secret, most sacred, the greatest of all mysteries. Its name is the book of the hidden dwelling–that is, the book of Amenta or the ritual of the resurrection. Obscure as these mysteries may seem, on account of the form– that of dramatic monologue and soliloquy–and the brevity of statement, we can recognize enough to know that these are the originals of all the other "mysteries", Gnostic, Kabalistic, Masonic, or Christian. The dogma of the incarnation was an Egyptian mystery. Baptismal regeneration, transfiguration, transubstantiation, the resurrection and ascension, were all Egyptian mysteries. The mystery of an ever– virgin mother; the mystery of a boy at twelve years of age transforming suddenly into an adult of thirty years, and then becoming one with the father, as it had been earlier in the mysteries of totemism; the mystery in which the dead body of Osiris is transubstantiated into the living Horus by descent of the bird–headed holy spirit; the mystery of a divine being in three persons, one of which takes flesh on earth as the human Horus, to become a mummy as Osiris in Amenta, and to rise up from the dead in spirit as Ra in heaven. These and other miracles of the Christian faith were already extant among the mysteries of Amenta. But the meaning of the mysteries could only be known whilst the genuine gnosis was authentically taught. This had ceased when the Christian Sarcolatræ took possession of the "Word–made– flesh", and literalized the mystical drama as a more tangible–looking human history, that was set forth in the very latest of the Gospels as a brand–new revelation sent from God, and personally conducted in Palestine by the "historic Jesus".

When Bendigo, the pugilist, became converted he proposed to take up preaching as his new profession. And when it was objected that he didn't know anything and couldn't read or write, he replied that he "expected to pick up a good deal by listening round". So was it with the early Christians. They could neither read nor write the ancient language, but they picked up a good deal by listening round. "You have your man upon the cross", said one of them to the Romans; "why do you object to ours?" Their man upon the cross being identical with Osiris– Tat or the ass–headed Iu. It is said of Taht as a teacher of the mysteries, "And now behold Taht in the secret of his mysteries. He maketh purifications and endless reckonings, piercing the firmament and dissipating the storms around him and so it cometh to pass that the Osiris hath reached every station", and, we may add, attained his immortality through the teachings communicated in the mysteries of Taht (Rit., ch. 130, Renouf). The 148th chapter of the Ritual recounts some of the most secret mysteries. It was written to furnish the gnosis or knowledge necessary for the Manes to get rid of his impurities and acquire perfection in the "bosom of Ra" the holy spirit.

At the entrance to the mysterious valley of the Tuat there is a walled–up doorway, the first door of twelve in the passage of Amenta. These twelve are described in the Book of Hades as twelve divisions corresponding to the twelve hours of darkness during the nocturnal journey of the sun. The first division has no visible door of entrance. The rest have open doors, and the twelfth has double doors. It is hard to enter, but made easy for the exit into the land of eternal life. Here is the mystery: how to enter where there is no door and the way is all unknown? I t is explained to the Manes how divine assistance is to be obtained. When the stains of life on earth are effaced the strength is given for forcing the entrance where there is no door, and in that power the Manes penetrates with (or as) the god (Rit., ch. 148, 2, 3). Thus Horus was the door in the darkness, the way where no entrance was seen, the life portrayed for the Manes in death. The secret entrance was one of the mysteries of Amenta. It was known as "the door of the stone", which name was given to their Necropolis by the people at Siut, the stone that revolved when the magical word or "open sesame" was spoken. The entrance to the Great Pyramid was concealed by means of a movable flagstone that turned on a pivot which none but the initiated could detect. This, when tilted up, revealed a passage four feet in breadth and three and a half feet in height into the interior of the building. This was a mode of entrance applied to Amenta as the blind doorway that was represented by the secret portal and movable stone of later legends. The means of entrance through what appeared to be a blank wall was by knowing the secret of the nicely-adjusted stone, and this secret was communicated to the initiates with the pass–word in the mysteries. Horus begins his work by carrying out the divine plans of his father Osiris on earth. He makes firm the battlements to protect Osiris against the assaults of all the powers of darkness. He makes the word of Osiris truth against his enemies. He opposes Sut, his father's adversary, to the death. He makes war upon the evil Apap, that old serpent, and overthrows the powers that rise up in rebellion, which are called the rebels in the Ritual, who are ever doomed to failure in the fight betwixt them and the father, who is now represented by Horus his beloved son, Horus of the resurrection, who is himself the door in death as the means of entrance to Amenta. He covers the naked body of the breathless one. He opens the fountains of refreshment for the god of the non–beating heart (ch. I). He wages battle on the "eater of the arm" (ch. II) and the black boar Sut, two types of the power of dearth, death, and darkness. He protects his father from the devouring crocodiles (ch. 32), from the serpents Rerek, Seksek, and Haiu, also from the apshait, an insect that preys upon the buried mummy (chs. 33, 34, 36). He says, "I have come myself and delivered the god in his dismembered condition. I have healed the trunk and fastened the shoulder and made firm the leg" (ch. 102), t..e., in reconstructing the mummy. He restores to Osiris his sceptre, his pedestal, and his staircase from the tomb (ch. 128). He says, "I have done according to the command that I should come forth in Tattu, to see Osiris" (ch. 78). He has kept the commandment that w as given him by the father. The Manes in Amenta tell of "the fortunes of that great son whom the father loveth", and how he had "pierced Sut to the heart", and how they had "seen the death". They also tell of the "divine plans which were carried out by Horus, in the absence of his father", when he represented Osiris on the earth (ch. 78). With his work accomplished, both on earth and in Amenta, Horus of the resurrection goes to see his father, and they embrace each other. Horus addresses his father, here called Ra–

Unnefer–Osiris–Ra. He exclaims: "Hail, Osiris ! I am thy son Horus; I have come. I have avenged thee. I have struck down thy enemies. I have destroyed all that was wrong in thee. I have killed him who assailed thee. I stretched forth my hand for thee against thy adversaries. I have brought thee the companions of Sut with chains upon them. I have ploughed for thee the fields. I have irrigated for thee thy land. I have hoed for thee the ground. I have built for thee the lakes of water. I have turned up the soil of thy possessions. I have made for thee sacrifices of thy adversaries. I have made sacrifices for thee of thy cattle and thy victims. I have bound thy enemies in their chains. I have sowed for thee wheat and barley in the field of Aarru. I have mowed them there for thee. I have glorified thee. I have anointed thee with the offering of holy oil. I have established for thee thy offerings of food on the earth for ever". (Rit., ch. 173, excerpt from Naville's rendering in Renouf's Book of the Dead.) All this and more he claims to have done. "I have given thee Isis and Nephthys". The twO divine sisters, the consorts of Osiris, the mothers and protectors of Horus, are thus brought back by him to the father. They have been with him from the beginning on earth in the hall of Seb; with him in his conception and incarnation by Isis and his nursing by Nephthys. They were his ministering angels, in attendance on him as protectors from the cut–throat Sut, or the monster Apap, who sought to slay the child or destroy it in the egg; with him in the agony of his blindness when torn and bleeding in the garden of Pa; with him as watchers in the tomb until he wakes; with him in his resurrection from Amenta. They are with him when he ascends to the father as conqueror of death, as ruler of the double earth and lord of the kingdom which he and his disciples or children have established for ever. The work attributed to Horus the divine exemplar, was to be fulfilled by his followers in the double earth of time and eternity. That was the object of the mysteries. It is in the character of the divine Horus that the human Nebseni says to Osiris, "Thou one God, behold me. I am Horus thy son. I have fought for thee. I have fought on thy behalf for justice, truth, and righteousness. I have overcome thine adversaries". He also claims to have done the things that Horus did as set forth in the writings or represented in the drama, and thus fulfilled the ideal of self–sacrificing sonship in very reality. making –the word of Osiris truth against his enemies. And it was but the word even when personified. which to be of any actual efficacy must be made truth in human life, in conduct. and in character (Pap. of Nebseni. Rit., ch. 173, Budge).

If there be any revelation or inspiration in a great ideal dramatically portrayed. the Egyptians found it in their divine model set forth in Horus :

> Horus the saviour, who was brought to birth
> As light in heaven and sustenance on earth.
> Horus in spirit, verily divine,
> Who came to turn the water into wine.
> Horus, who gave his life, and sowed the seed
> For men to make the bread of life indeed.
> Horus the comforter, who did descend
> In human fashion as the heavenly friend.
> Horus the word, the founder in his youth.
> Horus, fulfiller as the word made truth.
> Horus the lord and leader in the fight
> Against the dark powers of the ancient night.
> Horus the sufferer with his cross bowed down,
> Who rose at Easter with his double crown.
> Horus the pioneer, who paved the way
> Of resurrection to eternal day.
> Horus triumphant with the battle done,
> Lord of two worlds, united and made one.

It was the object of their loftiest desires to grow in his likeness whilst looking lovingly upon his features, listening to his word. and fulfilling his character in their own personal lives. A mythical model may be no more than an air-blown bladder for learning to swim by. The reality lies in learning to swim. This was how the ideal Horus served the Egyptians. They did not expect him to swim for them and carry them and their belongings as well but learned to swim for themselves.

There is nothing in all poetry considered as the flower of human reality more pathetic than the figure of Horus in Sekhem.He has grappled with the Apap of evil and wrestled with Sut–the de–vil or. Satan–and been overthrown in the passage of absolute darkne.s5. Blind and bleeding from many wounds. he continues to fight with death itself; he conquers, rises from the grave like a warrior with one arm! Not that he has lost an arm; he has only got one arm free from the bonds of death, the bandages of the mummy made for the burial. But he lives, he rises again triumphant, lifting the sign of the Dominator aloft; and in the next stage of transformation he will be altogether freed from the trammels of the mummy to become pure spirit, in the likeness of the father as the express image of his person.

It is a common Christian belief, continually iterated, that life and immortality were brought to light, and death, the last enemy, was destroyed, by a personal Jesus only nineteen centuries ago, whereas the same revelation had been accredited to Horus the anointed and to Iu–su the coming son for thousands of years before, with Horus or Iu–su as the impersonal and ideal revealer who was the Messiah in the astronomical mythology and the Son of God in the eschatology. The doctrine of immortality is so ancient in Egypt that the "Book of Vivifying the Soul for Ever"," said over a figure of the enlightened dead" , was not only extant some 6,000 years ago in the time of Husapti, fifth king of the first dynasty, it was then so old that the true tradition of interpretation was at that time already lost.The Egyptian Christ– Jesus or Horus, as revealer of immortality, was the ideal figure of a fact known to the ancient spiritualists, that the soul of man or the Manes persisted beyond death and the dissolution of the present body, and the drama of the mysteries was their *modus operandi* for teaching the fact, with Horus (or Iu–su) as typical manifestor. In this character he was set forth as the first fruits of them that slept, the only one that came forth from the mummy on earth, as the sahu mummy in Amenta; the only one, however, as a type that prefigured potential continuity for all, the doctrine being founded on the ghost as the phenomegal apparition of an eternal reality.

The Egyptians, who were the authors of the mysteries and mythical representation., did not pervert the meaning by an ignorant literalization of mystical matters, and had no fall of man to encounter in the fallacious Christian sense. Consequently they had no need of a redeemer from the effects of that which had never occurred. They did not rejoice over the death of their suffering saviour because his agony and shame and bloody sweat were falsely supposed to rescue them from the consequences of broken laws; on the contrary, they taught that everyone created his own karma here, and that the past deeds made the future fate. The morality was a thousandfold loftier and nobler than that of Christianity, with its delusive doctrine of vicarious atonement and propitiation by proxy. Horus did such or such things for the glory of his father, but not to save the souls of men from having to do them. There was no vicarious salvation or imputed righteousness. Horus was the justifier of the righteous, not of the wicked. He did not come to save sinners from taking the trouble to save themselves. He was an exemplar, a model of the divine sonship; but his followers must conform to his example, and do in life as he had done before they could claim any fellowship with him in death. Except ye do these things yourselves, there is no passage, no opening of the gate, to the land of life everlasting.

The Christian cult is often said to be founded on the "mysteries of the incarnation". But what teacher of the spurious mysteries has ever been able to tell us anything of their natural genesis? What has any bibliolator ever known about the word that was in the beginning? The word which issued out of Silence? The word of life that came by water, by blood, and in the Spirit? For him such language has never been related to any phenomena extant in nature. The wisdom of old Egypt only can explain the typical word and its relationship to a so-called revelation. The doctrine of the incarnation is Egyptian, and to the Egyptian wisdom we must appeal if we would understand it. No other word was ever made flesh in any other way than in Horus, who was the logos of the Mother Nature as the Child–Horus, the khart, or inarticulate logos, and the word that was made truth in the adult phase of his character as Horus Mat–Kheru, the second Horus, the

paraclete and direct representative of the father in heaven. The incarnation, which is looked upon as a central mystery of the Christian cult, had no origin and can have no adequate or proper explanation in Christianity. Its real origin, like those of the other

Egyptian dogmas and doctrines, was purely natural; it was prehistorical and non–personal, and as the mystery of Horus and his virgin mother, who were equally prehistorical and non–historical, it had been the central mystery of the Egyptian faith for ages, utilized by the ancient teachers for all it ever was or could be worth, and was continued by the teachers of historic Christianity in ignorance of its origin and only true significance, or with a criminally culpable suppression of the gnosis by which alone the inexplicable latter–day mysteries could have been explained.

The primitive mysteries were founded on the facts in nature which are verifiable today as from the first, whereas the mysteries of the Christian theology have been manufactured, shoddy–like, from the leavings of the past by the *modus operandi* of miracle. These remain today unverified because they are for ever unverifiable; We know how Horus came by water on his papyrus; how then did he come by blood? The child had been incorporated in the fish, the shoot, the branch, the beetle, calf, or Iamb, as the representative type; and in his incarnation, Horus came by blood, but not by the blood shed on a tree, or the tat–cross. He came to earth by blood as representative of the human soul that came by blood. The Ritual tells us that the gods issued out of silence (ch. 24): This was portrayed in the Osirian system when the infant Horus is depicted pointing with his finger to his mouth, making the sign of silence as it was understood in all the mysteries. Horus is not the ordinary child or khart of the hieroglyphics. He images the logos, the word of silence, the virgin's word, that gave a dumb or inarticulate utterance to the mystery of the incarnation. The doctrine of the incarnation had been evolved and established in the Osirian religion at least 4,000 and possibly 10,000 years before it was purloined and perverted in Christianity. It was so ancient that the source and origin had been forgotten and the direct means of proof lost sight of or obliterated except amongst the gnostics, who sacredly preserved their fragments of the ancient wisdom, their types and symbols and no doubt, with here and there a copy of some chapters of the Book of the Dead done into Greek or Aramaic by Alexandrian scribes. The doctrine of salvation by the blood of Isis connoted the idea of coming into existence by means of the mother's blood, or mystically the blood of the virgin mother. In primitive biology all birth and production of human life was first derived from the mother's blood, which was

afterwards informed by the soul of the fatherhood. The lesson first taught by nature was that life came by blood. Procreation could not occur until the female was pubescent. Therefore blood was the sign of source as the primary creative human element. Child–Horus came by the blood of the virgin Isis, in that and no other way. Jesus, the gnostic Christ, also came by blood that way, not only according to the secret doctrine of John, for the Musselmans have preserved a fragment of the true gnosis. In the notes to ch. 96 of the Koran, Sale quotes the Arabic tradition that Jesus was not born like any other men from blood concreted into flesh, but came *in the flow, or in the flowing blood*–that was, in the virgin's blood first personalized in Horus, who was made flesh as the virgin.'s child. The doctrine of the incarnation was dependent on the soul of life originating in the mother blood, the first that was held specifically and exclusively human on account of its incarnation. This was the soul derived from a mother who was the mystical virgin in biology, and who was afterwards mystified by theology as the mother of god, the eternal virgin typified in the likeness of the totemic. The blood mother had been cognized sociologically the virgin. Thence came the doctrine of a virgin mother as a type. Blood was the mother of a soul now differentiated from the external souls as human. First the white vulture of the virgin Neith, next the red heifer of the virgin Isis, then the human virginity, supplied the type of an eternal virgin, she in whom the mystery of maternal source was divinized as the virgin mother in the eschatology.

Thus "incarnation" proper begins with the soul that came into being by means of the virgin blood. This was the child of the mother only, the unbegotten Horus, w ho was an imperfect first sketch of the soul in matter that assumed the form of human personality as Horus the mortal, who as blind and maimed, deaf and dumb and impotent, because it was a birth of matter or the mother only, according to the mythical representation. The mother being the source and sustenance of life with her own blood, this led to a doctrine of salvation by the blood of Isis the divinized virgin. Thus the mystical blood mother was the earliest saviour, not the male. The elder Horus was her child who came by blood. He was her blood child in the eschatology; hence the calf, as his type, was painted red upon the tablets. As the Child–Horus he was an image of her suffering in the human form; thence Horus the child of blood became a saviour through suffering, in a mystery which had a natural origin. This origin can be followed in the Christian iconography when, as Didron shows, a figure of Jesus was portrayed upon the cross, as a little child of two years, naked, and with its body painted red all over, as was the Horus–calf upon the tablets. A curious instance of salvation by the blood of Isis is given in the Ritual. In a vignette to ch. 93, the saving and protecting power of the red tet–buckle, which is an image of the blood of Isis, is shown. A pair of human hands are outstretched from this amulet to grasp the arms of the Manes and prevent him from going toward the east, as that way lies the tank of flame, or hell in modern phrase. In the Gospel account of the incarnation the "word" was "made flesh", but the blood basis of the doctrine has been omitted. Salvation through the blood of Isis was imaged by the red tet–amulet that was put on by her when she had conceived her blood child. This salvation was effected when the child was brought into existence. According to the Ritual, the salvation of the Manes is in living–on hereafter. He pleads that he may live and be saved after death (ch. 41), and he wore the tet–buckle in his coffin as the sign of his salvation by the blood of Isis.

Further, how did a purificatory power come to be associated with blood so that one of the horrible dogmas of later theology could be expressed in lines like these :—

"There is a fountain filled with blood
Drawn from Immanuel's veins,
And sinners plunged beneath that flood
Lose all their guilty stains"?

The natural genesis of such a monstrous doctrine can be traced on two lines of descent. One of these has its starting–point in the theological victim being slain as a scapegoat in a sacrifice that was held to be piacular. The blood of the sin offering thus acquired the character of the atoning blood. According to the Christian doctrine, "All things are cleansed with blood, and apart from the shedding of blood there is no remission" (Heb. ix., 22). On the other line of descent, the idea of purification by blood was derived from a human origin, and not merely from the blood of the animal that was slain as a sacrifice for sin. This is one of the origins that were unfolded to the initiated by the teachers of the secret wisdom in the mysteries. The earliest form of the purifying blood was female. It was first the blood of the virgin mother, the blood of Isis, the blood of the incarnation, the flowing blood, the element in which Horus manifested when he came by blood, the blood on which the rite of purification was founded as a natural mode of cleansing. This is the one sole origin in the whole realm of nature for the blood which cleanseth, and it was in this feminine phase that a doctrine of purification by blood was established for the use of later theology when the sacrificial victim had been made a male who was held to have shed the atoning, purifying, saving blood upon a tree. There was no other way by which a soul was ever saved by blood than this act of salvation effected by the virgin mother. There never was any other incarnation than this of Horus in the blood of Isis, and no other saviour by blood was possible in the whole domain of unperverted nature. Neither could the transaction be made historical, nor the saviour personal, not if every tree on earth were cut into the figure of across with the effigy of a bleeding human body hung on every bough. Purification by means of blood then originated in the blood of Isis, the virgin mother of the human Horus, who, as the red child, calf or Iamb, personated that purification by blood which became doctrinal in the eschatology. To substitute the blood of a Jew shed on a cross as a means of making the purification for sins and the mode of cleansing souls in the "blood of the Iamb" for the natural purification of the mother was the grossest form of profanity, inconceivably impious to those who knew the mystical nature of the doctrine and its origin in human phenomena continued as a typical purification by blood that was practised in the mysteries, either by baptism or sprinkling with blood, or drinking blood, or eating the "bloody wafer" of the Roman eucharist. The natural blood sacrifice was feminine. The typical blood sacrifice was that of the red calf, the Iamb, or the child. The Iamb on the cross was the Christian victim until the eighth century A.D., at which time the man was permanently substituted for the Iamb, and the blood sacrifice was thenceforth portrayed as human and historical. A doctrine of voluntary sacrifice was founded from the time when the human mother gave herself to be eaten with honour by her children in the most primitive form of the mortuary meal. She offered her flesh to be eaten and her blood to be drunk; she gave herself as a natural blood sacrifice on which the typical was founded when the female totem as a cow, a bear, or other animal was made a substitute for the human mother. Also, when the earth was looked upon as the mythical mother of food and drink who was a wet–nurse in the water, and who gave herself bodily to her children for food, the sacrifice was typically continued if! totem ism when the animal supplied the sacramental food. As before shown, the earliest form of voluntary sacrifice was female. The human mother as victim was repeated in the mythology as divine, the mother in elemental nature; she who gave her flesh and blood as life to her children was then continued as a type in the more mystical phase. Hence came salvation by the blood of Isis–that is, by the virgin blood in which Horus was incarnated and made flesh, as the saviour who thus came by blood.

A Spaniard, who was paying expensively to regain the lost favour of the Holy Virgin, on being told by his priest that Mary had not yet forgiven him, is said to have shaken his fist in the face of his fetish and to have reminded her that she need not be so proud in her present position, as he had known her ever since she was only a bit of green plum tree. The ancient Egyptians knew the natural origins of their symbols and dogmas. Christians have mistaken the bit of green plum tree for an historical virgin.

The earliest form of god the father who became a voluntary sacrifice in Egypt was Ptah in the character of Sekari, the silent sufferer, the coffined one, the deity that opened up the nether–world for the resurrection in the solar mythos. As solar god he went down into Amenta. There he died and rose again, and thus became the resurrection and the way into a future lire as founder of Egyptian eschatology. Atum the son of Ptah likewise became the voluntary sacrifice as the source of life, but in another way and more apparent form. The mother human and divine had given life with her blood, and now the father, who was blended with the mother in Atum, is portrayed as creator of mankind by the shedding of his own blood.

In the cult of Ptah at Memphis and Atum at On there was a strenuous endeavour made to set creative source as male above the female. Hence it was said of the symbolic beetles that there was "no female race among them" (Hor–Apollo, B. I., 10). In cutting the member, Atum showed that he was the creator by the blood shed in a voluntary sacrifice. Male source is recognized, but according to what had preceded as the mother element, blood still remained a typical essence of creative life. And this is apparently illustrated by the rite of circumcision. The custom pertains, world over, to the swearing–in of the youths when they join the ranks of the fathers or begetters and follow the example of Atum as the father Ra, who was previously Horus the son. Atum, like Ptah, was also the typical sacrifice in the earth of eternity, who gave his life as sun god and as the master of food that sprang up for the Manes in Amenta. Osiris follows. In him the human mother who first gave herself to be eaten, and the great mother Isis, who was the saviour by blood, were combined with god the father in a more complete and perfect sacrifice as mother and father of the race in one. Lastly, the son as Horus or as

Iusa is made a vicarious sacrifice, not, however, as an atonement for sin, but as voluntary sufferer *instead* of his mother or his father. For in the Kamite scheme the mother never is omitted. Hence, when Horus comes in the character of the red god who orders the block of execution with the terrifying face of Har–Shefi. as the avenger of the afflictions suffered by his father (or by himself in his first advent), it is he " who lifteth up his father and who lifteth up his mother with his staff" (Rit., ch. 92, Renouf). Egypt, however, had anticipated Rome in attaining the "unbloody sacrifice" that was represented by the wafer, or loaf, of Horus as the bread of heaven, which took the place of flesh meat in the eucharistic meal, whilst retaining the beer or wine, as substitute for blood, in representing the female element. Thus Horus was eaten as the bread of life, and his blood was drunk in the red ale, or wine, as the final form in Egypt of the sacrificial, voluntary, living victim that had been the human mother, the typical mother, the totemic anima!, the cow of Hathor, the fish, the goose, the calf, the lamb, the victim in various forms, each one of which, down to the lentils and the corn, was figurative of the beneficent sacrifice that from the first was typical of a power in nature, call it mother or son, father, goddess or god, that provided food and drink, accompanied with an idea of sacrifice in the giving of life when blood was looked on as the life.

"How many sacraments hath Christ ordained in His Church?" is asked in the Prayer–book, and the answer is, "Two only as generally necessary to salvation–that is to say, baptism and the supper of the Lord". And both of these were Egyptian thousands of years earlier. The proof is preserved in that treasury of truth, the Ritual of the resurrection. In the first chapter of the Ritual (Turin Papyrus) it is said by the priest, "I lustrate with water in Tat tu and anoint with oil, in Abydos". We might call the Egyptians very particular Baptists for in the first ten gates of Elysium –or entrances to the great dwelling of Osiris the deceased is purified at least ten times over in ten separate baptisms, and ten different waters in which the gods and goddesses had been washed to make the water holy (Ritual, ch. 145). The inundation was the water of renewal to the life of Egypt, and this natural fact was the source and origin of a doctrine of baptismal regeneration. The salvation that came to Egypt in the Nile was continued in the Egyptian eschatology as salvation by water. ..I. give thee the liquid or humidity which ensures salvation", is said to the soul of the deceased (Rit., 155, I). They did not think that souls were saved from perdition by a wash of water or a bath of blood, but bodily baptism was continued as a symbol of purification for the spirit. The deceased explains that he had been steeped in the waters of natron and nitre, or salt, and made pure—pure in heart, pure in his forepart, his posterior part, his middle, and pure all over, so that there is no part of him remaining soiled or stained. The pool of baptism is dual in Amenta. In one part it is the pool of natron, in the other the pool of salt. Both natron and silt were used in preparing the mummy of the deceased, and the same process is repeated in the purification of the soul to make it also permanent, which was a mode of salvation. The deceased says, "May I be fortified or protected by seventy purifications" (Mariette, *Mon. divers*, pl. 63, I), just as Christians at the present time speak of being "fortified by the sacraments of the Church". "I purify myself at the great stream (the galaxy), where all my ills are made to cease; that which is wrong in me is pardoned, and the spots which were upon my body upon earth are washed away l' (Rit., ch. 86). "Lo, I come, that I may purify this soul of mine in the most high degree. Let me be purified in the lake of propitiation and of equipoise. Let me plunge into the divine pool beneath the two divine sycamores of heaven and earth" (ch. 97, Renouf). The pool of purification and healing that was figured in the northern heaven at the pole, and also reproduced in the paradise of Amenta, has been repeated in the Gospel according to John (ch. 5) as the Pool of Bethesda. In the Ritual (ch. 124, part 3) one of two waters is called the pool or tank of righteousness. In this pool the glorified elect receive their final purification and are healed. They are thus made pure for the presence of Osiris. The healing process was timed to take place at certain hours of the night or day. The Turin text gives the fourth hour of the night and the eighth hour of the day. But there are other readings. The Manes, as usual in the gospels, are represented by the "multitude of them that were sick, blind, halt, and withered", waiting to be healed. The elect or chosen ones are those who are first at the pool when the waters are troubled. Hence the story of the man who was non–elect.

It was a postulate of the Christians, maintained by Augustine and others, that infants who died unbaptized were damned eternally. This doctrine also had its rootage in the mysteries of Amenta. The roots have hitherto been hidden in the earth of eternity which has been mistaken for our earth of time. We are now enabled to exhibit them above ground and hold both root and product up to the light like the bulb of a hyacinth suspended in a glass water–bottle, These can now be studied, roots and all. The flesh that is formed of the mother's blood was held to share in the impurity of the female nature. It was in this sense solely that woman was the author of evil. The Child–Horus born of flesh and blood was the prototype of the unbaptized child–that is, the child unpurified by baptism. Without baptismal regeneration in Tattu there was no blending of the elder Horus with the soul or spirit of Horus divinized. According to the Egyptian doctrine, the development would be arrested and the soul from the earthly body might remain a wretched shade that was doomed to extinction, or, in the Christian perversion, was damned eternally. It was in Amenta that the dead were raised to inherit the second life. The resurrection had no other meaning for the Egyptians. And in the resurrection the Osiris is thus greeted: " Hail, Osiris ! thou art born twice! The gods say to thee: ' Come ! come forth; come see what belongs to thee in thy house of eternity' "(ch. 170). It is then that he is changed and renewed in an instant.

In blending the two halves of a soul that was dual in sex, dual also in matter and spirit, into one, according to the mystery of Tat tu, there was a return to the type beyond sex from which the two had bifurcated in the human creation. This one enduring soul was typical of the eternal soul which included motherhood and father–hood in one personality like that of the multi mammalian Osiris which the Child–Horus could only represent in some form of duality that imaged both sexes in one, as do the deities who are figured with one female bosom as a mode of en–onement. Female mummies have been exhumed that were made up wearing the beard of a male. This was another figure of the soul completed by uniting the two halves of sex in one figure, the type affected by the Queen Hatshepsu when she clothed herself in masculine attire and reigned as Mistress Aten. It was the same with the Pharaohs who wore the tail of the cow or lioness. They also included both halves of the perfect soul, as a likeness of the biune being divinized in heaven which they represented on the earth. The doctrine was brought on in the iconography of the gnostic artists when Jesus is figured as a woman with a beard, who is designated the Christ as Saint Sophia (or Charis) (Didron, fig. 50), and also when Jesus is depicted in the Book of Revelation as a being of both sexes, a youth with female paps; in the likeness of Osiris, whose male body is half covered with female mammæ, and who is Osiris in the upper and Isis in the lower part of the same mummy. Not only was it necessary to be regenerated and reborn in the likeness of god the father; the Manes could only enter the kingdom of heaven as a being of both sexes or of neither. The two halves of the soul that was established for ever in Tattu were male and female; the soul of Shu was male, the soul of Tefnut female. When these were united in one to form a completed Manes and a perfect spirit the result was a typical creation from both sexes in which there was neither male nor female. This oneness, in the Horus who was divinized, is the oneness in Christ described by Paul "As many of you as were baptized into Christ, did put on Christ. There can be no male nor female, for ye are all one in Christ Jesus". One of the fragments preserved by Clement Alexander and Clement of Rome from the lost gospel of the Egyptians, which is more than fully recoverable in the Ritual, will show the continuity of the doctrine as Egyptian in a gospel that was designated "Egyptian". The Lord having been asked by Salome when his kingdom would come, replied, "when you shall have trampled under foot the garment of shame; When two shall be one, when that which is without shall be like that which is within, and when the male with the female shall be neither male nor female". The "garment of shame" was feminine, being as it was of the flesh. On this the Ritual has a word to say. The impurity of matter which came to be ascribed to the mother of all flesh, or female nature, is symbolically shown in the chapters for arranging the funeral bed (Rit., chs. 170–171). This is exemplified by means of the feminine garment–the apron–which is here considered to be a sign of all that was wrong in the deceased; the wrong that was derived from the mother, as elsewhere described in the Ritual, because it is the garb of impurity called "the garment of shame" in the Egyptian gospel, which was to be trampled under foot when the male and female were to be made one in spirit, or as spirit. In the ceremony of "wrapping up the deceased in a pure garment", the impure one being now discarded is alluded to in ch. 172. When the deceased was stretched upon the funeral bed the body was *divested of the apron* and clothed in the pure garment of the khus or spirits, " the pure garment allotted to him for ever" (Rit., ch. 171). But the feminine garment is still worn without shame by the masquerading male as the bishop's apron, which can be traced back as feminine to the loin–cloth and apron first worn by the sex for the most primitive and pitiful of human needs at the time of puberty. The bishop in his apron, like the priest in his petticoat and the clergyman in his surplice, is a likeness of the biune being who united both sexes in one; the modern Protestant equivalent for the Pharaoh with the cow's tail, and Venus with a beard, the mutilated eunuch, or any other dual type

of hermaphrodital deity. Men who masquerade in women's clothing are commonly prosecuted, but the bishop carries on his mummery without even being suspected. He walks about as ignorant of his vestmental origins as any of the passers by. Usually the custom of men dressing in women's clothing is limited to our Easter pastimes, but the bishops still carry it on all through the year.

The Christians prattle about the divine "sonship of humanity", manifested in the historical Jesus. But they have no divine daughtership, no origin for the soul as female and no female soul. The Jews did all they could to get rid of the female part of the divine nature, and the exigency of the Christian history has suppressed the feminine element altogether in the human type that represented both sexes in humanity as it was set forth by the Egyptians in the mysteries. Finally, it has been frequently asserted that only through the Gospel Jesus has a god of the poor man ever been revealed– a statement most profoundly false. A god of the poor and suffering was personified in Horus the elder. But there is a corollary to the character. He is likewise an avenger of the sufferings. Horus at Edfu is said to protect the needy against the powerful. Also, in the great Judgment Hall the Osiris deceased upon his trial says, "I have not been a land–grabber. I have not exacted more than should be done for me as the first fruits of each day's work" (Rit. ch. 125). Various other statements tend to show that the unjust capitalists of those times had a mortal dread of facing Osiris the divinized judge, who was likewise god of the poor and needy. In an Egyptian hymn the one god, Atum the maker of men, is described as "lying awake while all men lie asleep, to seek out the good of his creatures" (line 12), "listening to the poor in their distress, gentle of heart when one cries to him. Deliverer of the timid man from the violent, lord of mercy most loving, judging the poor, the poor and the oppressed" (Hymn to Amen–Ra, *Records*, vol. ii., p. 129). Taht was the recorder in the Judgment Hall. At the weighing of hearts he portrayed the character of the deceased, and in one of the texts it is said that when he placed the heart in the scales against Maati, the goddess of justice, he leaned to the side of mercy, that the judgment might be favourably inclined, as though he exerted a little pressure on the human side of the balance.

It has also been said that the historic Jesus came to glorify the lot of labour, which antiquity despised, whereas the Egyptian paradise was the reward of labour, and Horus the husbandman in the harvest–

field of the Aarru is the worker, personified. No one attained the Egyptian heaven but the worker, who reaped solely in proportion as he had sown. The portion of land allotted to the Manes for cultivation in Amenta was enlarged only for those who had been good labourers on earth. The Shebti figures in the tombs are equipped for labour with the plough or hoe in their hands. As agriculturists they put their hands to the plough. There was no unearned increment for loafers in the earth of eternity. A flash of revelation lightens from the cloud of Egypt's past when we learn from the Ritual that a part of the work to be performed in the Aarru paradise or field of harvest in Amenta was to clear away the life–choking sand. These fighters and conquerors of the much. detested desert still retain that image of the earliest cultivators, the makers of the soil which they enclosed and first protected from the drifting, sterilizing sand. The Manes, addressing the Shebti figures, says to them, "O typical ones! If I should be judged worthy of doing the work that has to be done in Amenta, bear witness for me that I am worthy to fertilize the fields, to flush the streams, and transport the sand from west to east" (Rit., ch. 6). He became one of the glorified elect in being judged worthy of the work. This will show that in making the primeval paradise they were still the cultivators who had conquered on earth by their long wrestle with the powers of dearth in the desert when they made their passage through the wilderness of sand and held on to the skirts of Mother Nile, who led them to a land which she herself had made for them to turn into an oasis and a paradise of plenty with her waters for assistance in the war against Apap, or Sut, the Sebau, and the burning Sahara. It may also explain why the Pharaohs from the time of the eleventh dynasty were officially entitled "Masters of the Oasis", the oasis, that is, which had been created in Egypt by human labour to be localized in Amenta as the promised land that was to be attained at last among the never–setting stars in the oasis of eternity.

The prototypes of hell and purgatory and the earthly paradise are all to be found in the Egyptian Amenta. There is, says the Christian rhymer, Dr. Watts

> "There is a dreadful hell
> And everlasting pains,
> Where sinners must with devils dwell
> In darkness, fire, and chains".

The darkness, fire, and chains, as well as the brimstone, which was the stone of Sut, and other paraphernalia of the Christian hell, are also Egyptian.

But the chains were employed for the fettering of Sut, the Apap, and the Sebau, the evil adversaries of Osiris, the good or perfect being, not for the torturing of souls that once were human. The Egyptian hell was not a place of everlasting pain, but of extinction For those who were wicked irretrievably. It must be admitted, to the honour and glory of the Christian deity, that a god of eternal torment is an ideal distinctly Christian, to which the Egyptians never did attain. Theirs was the all–parental god, Father and Mother in one whose heart was thought to bleed in every wound of suffering humanity, and Whose son was represented in the character of the Comforter.

Also the hell–fire of Christian theology, the hell–fire that is unquenchable (Mark ix. 43, 44), is a survival of the representation made in the Egyptian mysteries. The Osiris in Amenta passes through this hell of fire in "which those who are condemned suffer their annihilation. He says, "I enter in and I come forth from the tank (or lake) of flame on the day when the adversaries are annihilated at Sekhem" (Rit., ch. I). When the glorified deceased had made his voyage in heaven "over the leg of Ptah" and reached the mount of glory, he exclaims, "I have come from the lake of flame, from the lake of fire and from the field of flame". He has made his escape from destruction, and attained the eternal city at the pole of heaven. This lake of fire that is never quenched was derived from the solar force in the mythology on which the eschatology was based. Hence the locality was in the east, at the place of sunrise. The wicked were consumed by fire at the place where the righteous entered the solar bark to sail the heavenly waters called the Kabhu, or the cool, and voyage west– ward toward the heaven of the setting stars. The lake of flame was in the east, the lake of outer darkness in the west. For when the bark of Ra or the boat of souls had reached the west at sunset there was a great gulf fixed between the mount called Manu in the west and the starry vault of night, the gulf of Putrata (Rit., ch. 44), where the dead fell into darkness unless supported by Apuat the star–god, by Horus in the moon, and by Ra the solar deity, the visible representatives of superhuman powers in the astronomical mythology.

At the "last judgment" in the mysteries those who had failed to make the word of Osiris truth against his enemies, as the formula runs, were doomed to die a second death. The first was in the body on the earth, the second in the spirit. The enemies of justice, law, truth, and right were doomed to be destroyed for ever in the lake of fire or tank of flame. They were annihilated once for all (Rit., ch. I). The doctrine crops up in the Pauline Epistles and in Revelation, where the end of all is \with a destruction in the lake of fire. In the Epistle to the Hebrews the destruction of lost souls is compared \with that of vegetable matter being consumed by fire. The doctrine, like so many others, was Egyptian, upon \which the haze of ignorance settled down, to cause confusion ever since. Take away the Kamite devil, and the Christian world \mould suffer sad bereavement. The devil was of Egyptian origin, both as "that old serpent" the Apap reptile, the devil \with a long tail, and as Sut, w ho was Satan in ananthropomorphic guise. Sut, the power of drought and darkness in physical phenomena, becomes the dark–hearted evil one, and is then described as causing storms and tempests, going round the horizon of heaven II like one whose heart is veiled" (Rit., ch. 39, Renouf), as the adversary of Osiris the Good Being. The darkness, fire, and chains are all Egyptian. Darkness was mythically represented by the Apap dragon, also as the domain of Sut in the later theology. Darkness in the nether world is identical with the tunnels of Sut in Amenta. The chains are likewise Egyptian, but not for human wear. Apap and the Sebau, Sut and the Sami are bound in chains. It is said to the pre–anthropomorphic devil, "Chains are cast upon thee by the scorpion goddess" (Rit., ch. 39).

Sut is also imprisoned with a chain upon his neck (ch. 108). As already explained, the Sebau and the Sami represent the physical forces in external nature that made for evil and were for ever opposed to the Good Being and to the peace of the world. These were always rising in impotent revolt as the hosts of darkness and spawn of Apap, headed by the evil-hearted Sut. They had to be kept under; hence the necessity for prisons, bonds, and chains. The mythical imagery has been continued in the Christian eschatology, and the sinners put in the place of the Sebau, whereas in the Egyptian teaching the sinners, once human, who were irretrievably bad, were put an end to once for all, at the time of the second death, in the region of annihilation (Rit., ch. 18). Coming to an end for ever was, to the Egyptian mind, a prospect worse than everlasting pains, so profound was their appreciation of life, so powerful their will to persist. They represented evil as negation.

Apap is evil and a type of negation in the natural phenomena that were opposed to good. In the eschatology Sut represents negation as nonexistence. Evil culminated in annihilation and non–being for the Manes, and the negation of being, of life, of good, was the ultimate form of evil. The Egyptian purgatory, called the Meskat, is a place of purgation where the primitive mode of purifying may be compared with that of Fulling. It is effected by beating. Hence the Meskat is the place of scourging. The Manes pleads that he may not fall under the knives of the executioners in the place of extermination, as he has "*passed* through the place of purification in the middle of the Meskat". In chapter 72 the Manes prays that he may "not be stopped at the Meskat", or in purgatory, but may pass on to the divine dwelling–place prepared for him by Tum "above the earth", where he can "join his two hands together", and eat the bread and drink the beer upon the table of Osiris. The same plea, "Let me not be stopped at the Meskat", or kept in purgatory , is also uttered by the speaker in chapter 99. The enemies of the Good Being were likewise pilloried. Hence the Manes says, "Deliver me from the gods of the pillory. who fasten (the guilty) to their posts" (ch. 180).

A late attempt has been made on behalf of the Roman Catholic religion to lure people into Hades by showing that it is only a mitigated mourning department; that the devil himself is not so black as hitherto painted, and that there is really a tolerable amount of happiness to be obtained in hell. But this is only looking a little closer into the traditions of Amenta which survived in Rome.They belong to the same original source as that from which the Church derived its doctrines of purgatory, the second death, and other dogmas not to be found in the Gospels. There is no everlasting bonfire of eternal torture in the Egyptian hells, of which there are ten, known as the ten circles of the condemned, in the inferno or divine nether region. The utterly worthless suffer a second death upon the highways of the damned, and are spoken of as those who are no more. The Roman Church continued the dogma of a second death, and then somewhat nullified it by adding punishment of an infinite duration, as being more coercive to all who did or did not zealously believe. There was no other identifiable source for the Christian eschatology than the Egyptian wisdom. The Roman Church was founded on the Ritual. Possibly a version of the original may one day be found preserved in the secret archives of Rome, the text of which would explain numerous pictures in the Catacombs and other works of the gnostic artists who were the actual authors of the Egypto–Christian iconography, not the "few poor fishermen". The Roman Church will yet find that she is at root Egyptian, and will then seek to slough off the spurious history which by that time will be looked upon as solely incremental.

The Egyptians were the greatest realists that ever lived. For thousands and thousands of years it was their obvious endeavour at full stretch to reach the ultimate reality of eternal truth. Their interrogation of nature was like the questioning– of children, very much in earnest: "But is it really true?" The real was the quest of their unceasing inquiry. To be real was the end and aim; that was living in truth. The only one god was the real god. Horus in spirit was the real Horus. Reality was royalty. In the time of the fifth dynasty a certain Tep–en–ankh claims to be "the *real* judge and scribe", the "*real* nearest friend of the king". For them eternal life was the ultimate reality. The Egyptian was pre–eminently a manly religion, and therefore calculated to develop manhood. In the hall of the last judgment the deceased expects justice and equity. His god is a just and righteous judge. He does not pray for mercy or writhe in the dust to seek a sentimental forgiveness for sins, or sue for clemency. His was not a creed of that nature. He knows it is the life, the character, the conduct that will count in the scales of Maati for the life hereafter. The human Horus put in no plea for sinners on account of his sufferings. Divine Horus throws no make–weight into the scale. Deceased is judged by what he has done and by what he has not done in the life on earth. He must be sound at heart. He must have spoken and acted the truth. The word of god must have been made truth by him to be of any avail at the bar of judgment. That was the object of all the teaching in all the mysteries and writings which were held to be divine. The standard of law without and within was set up under the name of Maati or Maat, a name denoting the fixed, undeviating law and eternal rule of right. Hence the same word signifies law, truth, justice, rightfulness, and the later righteousness. The foremost and the final article of the Egyptian creed was to fulfil Maati. This is the beginning, the middle, and the end of the moral law. The deity enthroned by them for worship was the god of Maati, tile name, which has the fourfold meaning of law, justice, truth, and right, which are one as well as synonymous. Judgment with justice was their aim, their alpha and omega, in administering the law which their religious sense had divinized for human use; and its supreme type, erected at the pole, in the equinox, or the Hall of Judgment, was the pair of scales at perfect equipoise, for with them the equilibrium of the universe was dependent on eternal equity.

It may look like taking a flying leap in the dark to pass from the Egyptian Book of the Dead to Bunyan's *Pilgrim's Progress*, but whencesoever Bunyan derived the tradition, the *Pilgrim's Progress* contains all outline of the matter in the Egyptian Ritual. Christian personates the Manes on his journey through the nether earth, with the roll in his hand containing the word of life. The escape from the City of Destruction may be seen in the escape of the deceased from the destruction threatened in Amenta, when he exclaims. "I come from the lake of flame, from the lake of fire and from the field of flame" (ch. 98). The wicket–gate corresponds to the secret doorway of the mysteries; the "Slough of Despond" to the marshes in the mythos; the "Hill Difficulty" to the Mount of Ascent up which the Osiris climbs with "his staff in his hand". The Manes forgets his name; Christian forgets his roll, the roll that was his guide book for the journey and his passport to the celestial city. The prototypal valley of the shadow of death is the Aar–en–tet in Amenta. This is the valley of darkness and death (Rit., ch. 19; 13, 6). The Ritual says, "Let not the Osiris advance into the valley of darkness" where the twice–dead were buried for ever by the great annihilator Seb. The monster Apap is the original Apollyon. The equipment of Christian in his armour for his conflict \with Apollyon in the Valley of Humiliation is one with the equipment of the Osiris, who enters the valley "glorious and well equipped" for the battle with his adversary the dragon. The fight of Christian and Apollyon is identical \with the contest between Ra and Apap. All the time of his struggle Apollyon fought with yells and hideous roarings; Apap with "the voice of strong bellowings " (Rit., ch. 39). Christian passes by the mouth of hell; the Osiris passes by the ten hells, with all of them, as it were, making mouths at him for their prey. There are two lions at the gate of the Palace Beautiful, and in the Ritual the two lions crouch at the beautiful gate of exit from Amenta (Vig. to ch. 18). The waters of the river of life, the green meadows, the delectable mountains, the land of Beulah, the paradise of peace, the celestial city on the summit, all belong to the mythology of Hetep or the Mount of Glory–a bare outline, the mere skeleton of which has been clothed at different times in various forms, including this of the *Pilgrim's Progress*. Possibly Bunyan the tinker derived the tradition from those travelling tinkers the gipsies. However this may be, the Egyptian Ritual is the verifiable source of Bunyan's *Pilgrim's Progress*.

Many illustrations might also be given to show that the mysteries of Amenta, which were finally summed up as "Osirian", have been carried to the other side of the world. In the mythology of the aborigines of New Holland, "Grogoragally, the divine son, is the active agent of his father, who immovably presides over all nature (like Osiris, the mummy god of the motionless heart). The son watches the actions of men, and quickens the dead immediately upon their earthly interment. He acts as mediator for the souls to the great god, to whom the good and bad actions of all are known. His office is chiefly to bring at the close of every day the spirits of the dead from all parts of the world to the judgment–seat of his father, where alone there is eternal light. There he acts as intercessor for those who have only spent some portion of their lives in wickedness. Bayma, listening to the mediation of his son, allows Grogoragally to admit some such into Ballima, "or heaven (Manning, *Notes on the Aborigines of New Holland*, Sydney, 1883, copy from the author). Grogoragally is one with the hawk–headed Horus, the paraclete or advocate who pleads for the Manes before the judgment–seat of his father. Again, the aborigines of the McDonnell Ranges have a tradition that the sky was at one time inhabited by three persons. One of these was a woman, one was a child who always remained a child and never developed beyond childhood; the third was a man of gigantic stature called Ulthaana–that is a spirit. He had an enormous foot shaped like that of an emu. When a native dies he is said to ascend to the home of Ulthaana the spirit (Gillen, *Notes, Horn Expedition*, vol. iv., p. 183).

This is a far–off folk tale that may be traced back home to the Egyptian myth. In this Child–Horus never developed beyond childhood, and so remained the eternal child. This was Horus of the incarnation who made his transformation into the Horus that rose again as the adult, the great man, Horus in spirit, the prototype of "Ulthaana". The bird type is repeated. Horus has the head of the hawk, as a figure of the man in spirit;. Ulthaana, as a spirit, has the foot of an enormous emu.

The Arunta also have a kind of Amenta or world of spirits under ground. About fourteen miles to the south of Alice Springs there is a cave in a range of hills which rises to the north. This cave, like all others in the range, is supposed to be occupied by the Iruntarinia or spirit individuals, each one of whom is in reality the double of one of the ancestors of the tribe who lived in the Alcherinf!a. The individual spirits are supposed to live within the cave in perpetual sunshine and among streams of running water, as in the Egyptian meadows of Aarru. Here, as in Amenta, the reconstitution of the deceased takes place. Within the cave the Iruntarinia remove all the internal organs, and provide the man with a completely new set, after which operation has been successfully performed he presently comes to life again, but in a condition of insanity. This, however, is of short duration, and the coming round is equivalent to the recovery of memory by the Manes in the Ritual, when he remembers his name and who he is in the great house of the other world (Spencer and Gillen, p. 525). There are bird–souls also in this nether earth, which are favoured with unlimited supplies of down or undattha, with which they are fond of decorating their bodies as spirits. The mysteries of Amenta are more or less extant in the totemic ceremonies of the Central Australians at a more rudimentary stage of development, which means, according to the present reading of the data, that the same primitive wisdom was carried out from the same central birthplace in Africa to the islands of the Southern Sea, and there fossilized during long ages of isolation, which had been carried down the Nile to take living root and grow and flourish as the mythology and eschatology of ancient Egypt.

In the mysteries of Amenta the deceased is reconstructed from seven constituent parts or souls in seven stages of development. Corresponding to these in the Arunta mysteries, seven "status–terms are applied to the initiate". (1) He is called Ambaquerka up to the time of his being tossed in the air. (2) He is Ulpmerka until taken to the circumcision ground. (3) He is the Wurtja during the time betwixt being painted for it and the actual performance of the ceremony. (4) He is Arakurta betwixt the operations of circumcision and sub–incision. (5) He is Ertwa–kurka after circumcision until he passes through the ordeal by fire. (6) Following this he is called Illpongwurra, and (7) after passing through the engwurra he is designated Urliara. (Spencer and Gillen, N. T., p. 638.) In the mysteries of Amenta the mouth of the resuscitated spirit is opened and the silence of death is broken when the lips are touched by the sacred implement in the hands of Ptah.

It is said in the "ceremony of opening the mouth", "Let my mouth be opened by Ptah with the instrument of ba–metal with which he openeth the mouths of the gods" (ch. 23). The Arunta also perform the ceremony of opening the mouth by touching it with a sacred object when the initiates are released from the ban of silence (Spencer and Gillen, pp. 382, 385). A mystery of the resurrection is acted by the Arunta in the *quabarra ingwurninga inkinja*, or corroborree of the arisen bones, which bones imaged the dead body, whilst the performers represented the Ulthaana or spirits of the dead (p.473). The bones were sacredly preserved by those who were as yet unable to make the mummy as a type of permanence.

Messrs. Spencer and Gillen tell us that every Australian native has to pass through certain ceremonies before he is admitted to the secrets of the tribe. The first takes place at about the age of ten or twelve years, whilst the final and most impressive one is not passed through until probably *the native has reached the age of at least twenty–five, or It may be thirty years* " (*N. T.*, pp. 212, 213). These two initiations correspond to those in the mysteries of the double Horus. At twelve years of age the Child–Horus makes his transformation into the adult in his baptism or other kindred mysteries. Horus as the man of thirty years is initiated in the final mystery of the resurrection. So was it with the gnostic Jesus. The long lock of Horus, the sign of childhood, was worn by him until he attained the age of twelve years, when he was changed into a man. With the southern Arunta tribe the hair of the boy is for the first time tied up at the commencement of the opening ceremony of the series by which he is made a man. HIS long hair is the equivalent of the Horus lock. The first act of initiation in the Arunta mysteries is that of throwing the boy up into the air–a ceremony that still survives with us in the tossing of the new–comer in a blanket! This was a primitive mode of dedication to the ancestral spirit of the totem or the tribe, whose voice is heard in the sound of the churinga or bull–roarer whirling round. It is said by the natives that the voice of the great spirit was heard when the resounding bull–roarer spoke. The great spirit was supposed to descend and enter the body of the boy and to make him a man, just as in the mystery of Tat tu the soul of Horus the adult descends upon and unites with the soul of Horus the child, or the soul of Ra the holy spirit descends upon Osiris to quicken and transform and re–erect the mummy. Where risen Horus becomes bird–headed as the adult in spirit the Arunta youth is given the appearance of flight to signify the change resulting from the descent of the spirit as the cause of transformation. When one becomes a soul in the mysteries of the Ritual by assuming the form or image of Ra, the initiate exclaims "Let me wheel round in *whirls*, let me *revolve* like the *turning one* " (ch. 83). The" turning one" is the sun god Chepera (Kheper), whose name is identical with that of an Australian tribe. Kheper is the soul of "self–originating force" that was imaged under one type by the bennu, a bird that ascends the air and flies to a great height whilst circling round and round in spiral wheels (Rit., ch. 85).

Whether this be the churinga, the bribbun, turndun, or whirler in a glorified form or not, the doctrine of soul-making at puberty is the same in the Australian as in the Egyptian mysteries.

In the Egyptian mythology Horus is the blind man, or rather he is the child born blind, called Horus in the dark. He is also described as the blind Horus in the city of the blind. In his blindness he is typical of the emasculated sun in winter and of the human soul in death. At the place of his resurrection or rebirth there stands a tree up which he climbs to enter spirit life. And we are told that "near to Charlotte Waters is the tree that Jose to mark the spot where a blind man died". This tree is called the *apera okilchya* – that is, the blind man's tree, and the place where it stands was the camp of the blind, the city of the blind, the world of the dead, in which the tree of life or dawn was rooted (N.T., p. 552). Should the tree be cut down the men where it grows will become blind. They would be like Horus in the dark, this being the tree of light or the dawn of eternal day. In one of their ceremonies the Arunta perform the mystery of the oruncha which existed in the Alcheringa. These were evil spirits or "devil-devil men", malevolent and murderous to human beings, especially to the women after dark (N.T., p. 329,331, 390–1). In this performance they are portrayed as prowling round, crawling, peering about, and seeking whom they may devour. They run backwards and forwards on all fours as beasts of prey, growling and pretending to frighten each other. The oruncha are the creatures of the dark, with horns like the mediæval devil, and they correspond to the Sebau fiends or evil spirits of the Egyptian mythos who are the enemies of the good Osiris in Amenta. These devil–devil men made war upon the lizard men, the men of the lizard totem, but there were two brothers who rushed upon them as avengers, and slew the whole of the oruncha. The evil powers were the creatures of chaos, the spawn of darkness, the devils of drought, with whom there was no law or order. The two brothers = brotherhoods belonged to the lizard totem, together with their wives. This was the earliest totem of the Arunta.

In the last of the initiation ceremonies the Arunta raise a special mound, called the parra, on the engwura ground, where the final rites are performed and full initiation is attained. Here the nurtunga was raised, and the parra mound was, so to say, erected at the pole. Messrs. Spencer and Gillen tell us they were unable to learn the meaning of the word parra. But, as the comparison is not simply verbal, we note that para is an ancient Egyptian name for Annu, the place of the column, the mount of the pole, and of the balance in the Maat. The Chepara tribe of Southern Queensland also throw up the circular mound for their greater mystery of the kuringal, in which may be identified the baptism and rebirth by fire (Howitt, *Australian Ceremonies of the Initiation*). Amongst the initiatory rites of the Arunta mysteries is the purification by fire. When the initiate has passed through this trial he becomes a perfectly developed member of the tribe, and is called an urliara, or one who has been proved by fire (*N.T.*, p. 271).The natives say that the ceremony has the effect of strengthening the character of all who pass through it. This is one of the most obvious survivals. Afire ceremony is described in the Ritual as an exceeding great mystery and a type of the hidden things in the under world. It is an application of the fires by means of which power and might are conferred upon the spirits (khu) among the stars which never set. These fires, it is said in the rubric (ch. 137 , A), shall make the spirit as vigorous as divine Osiris. It is a great ordeal, and so secret is the mystery that it is only to be seen by the males. "Thou shalt not perform this ceremony before any human being, except thine own self or thy father or thy son". Amongst other things the fire is good for destroying evil influences and for giving power to Horus in his war with darkness. It is of interest to note the part played by the females in the ordeals by fire. In one of these the fire is prepared by the women, and when the youth squats upon the fire they place their hands upon his shoulder and gently press him down upon the smoking fuel (N.T., p. 259). Now in the Egyptian mysteries of Amenta the punishers or purifiers in the hells or furnaces are women or goddesses, and it looks as if this character had survived in the mysteries of the Arunta. When the elders shout through the darkness to the women across the river, "What are you doing? " the reply is, " We are making a fire". " What are you going to do with the fire?" is asked, and the women shout, "We are going to burn the men". This occurs during a pause by night in the ceremonies of initiation, which terminate with the ordeal by fire. (Spencer and Gillen.) The concluding ordeals by fire and the "final washing" in the Australian ceremonies can be paralleled in the Ritual. "Lo, I come", says the speaker, "that I may purify this soul of mine in the most high degree" (ch. 97); and again, "I come from the lake of flame, from the lake of fire and from the field of flame, and I live". He is now a spirit sufficiently advanced to join the ancient never– setting ones and become a fellow–citizen with them in the eternal city (ch. 98). The initiate in the Australian mysteries having passed through the initiatory ceremonies, joins the elders as a fully–developed member of his tribe.

The most sacred ceremonial object of the Arunta is called the kaltaua. This is erected at the close of the engwura mysteries. A young gum–tree, 20 feet in height, is cut down, stripped of its branches and its bark, to be erected in the middle of the sacred ground. The decoration at the top was "just that of a human head". It was covered allover with human blood, unless red ochre had been substituted. The exact significance of the kauaua is not known to the natives, but, as the writers affirm, it has some relation to a human being, and is regarded as common to the members of all the totems (p.630). Its mystery is made known at the conclusion of the engwura, a series of ceremonies, the last of the initiatory rites through which the native must pass to become a fully–developed member who is admitted to all the secrets of the tribe, of which this is apparently final and supreme. All things considered, we think the sacred kauaua is a form of the Egyptian ka–statue, which is a type of eternal duration as an image of the highest soul. To make the kauaua, so to say, the pole is humanized. It is painted with human blood, and ornamented like the human head. It has but one form, and is common to all the totems. So is it with the

Egyptian ka, the eidolon of the enduring soul. The name of the kauaua answers to a long–drawn–out form of the word "ka", as ka–a–a. The mysteries of the Arunta, which sometimes take four months together for a complete performance, constitute their religious ceremonies, their mean of instruction, their books, their arts of statuary, painting, and Sign–language, their modes of preserving the past, whether lived on earth, or, as they have it, in the Alcheringa, during the times of the mythical ancestors beyond which tradition does not penetrate. The main difference betwixt the Australian and the Egyptian mysteries is that the one are performed on this earth in the totemic stage of sociology, the other in the earth of Amenta in the phase of eschatology. Also the Egyptians continued growing all the time that the Australians were standing still or retrograding. Lastly, we may be sure that such mysteries as these did not spring from a hundred different origins and come together by fortuitous concourse from the ends of the earth, to be finally formulated as the Egyptian mysteries of Amenta.